ALIEN ENCOUNTERS

ALIEN ENCOUNTERS

ANATOMY
OF
SCIENCE
FICTION

MARK ROSE

Harvard University Press
Cambridge, Massachusetts
London, England   1981

Library of Congress Cataloging in Publication Data

Rose, Mark.
    Alien encounters.

    Includes bibliographical references and index.
    1. Science fiction – History and criticism.   I.   Title.
PN3433.8.R6   809.3'876   81-683
ISBN 0-674-01565-7   AACR2

To Rachel, Jonah, and Teddy

ACKNOWLEDGMENTS

I am indebted to the National Endowment for the Humanities for a Fellowship that allowed me to complete this book, and to the University of California, Santa Barbara, for clerical and research support. A few paragraphs that originally appeared in my *Science Fiction: A Collection of Critical Essays*, Twentieth Century Views (Englewood Cliffs: Prentice-Hall, 1976), have been reworked and included in this book. I have also incorporated a small amount of material that was originally published in *The New Republic*. Many friends and colleagues discussed sections of the work with me and assisted or encouraged me in other ways. I hope my failure to mention them by name will not be taken as a sign of ingratitude. Still I wish to thank Karen Cunningham and Jeffrey Hudson, who helped with my research.

The Wallace Stevens epigraph is from "Notes Toward a Supreme Fiction," *The Collected Poems of Wallace Stevens*, copyright 1954 by Wallace Stevens (Alfred A. Knopf, Inc.).

CONTENTS

From this the poem springs: that we live in a place
That is not our own.

— Wallace Stevens

GENRE

In 1967 the British science-fiction magazine *New Worlds* published a story by Pamela Zoline, "The Heat Death of the Universe," which has since become something of a minor classic. Zoline's title invokes expectations of cosmic cataclysm of a sort familiar in science fiction. But the story merely narrates the difficulties of a California housewife's day, counterpointing descriptions of Sarah Boyle serving breakfast, washing diapers, watering plants, and shopping for a birthday party with an exposition of the second law of thermodynamics and the principle of entropy. The cosmic heat death of the title – if the universe is a closed system, it must be moving toward a state when eventually no energy will be available – becomes a metaphor for the condition of Sarah Boyle's life, and when this has been established the story stops. An interesting piece of fiction, and one that clearly gains resonance and impact by having been published in a context of science-fiction expectations. But is it science fiction?

"The Heat Death of the Universe" raises once again, and in a particularly provocative manner, a problem that seems to bedevil everyone who thinks seriously about science fiction. What is it anyway? Is *Gulliver's Travels* science fiction? Is *Frankenstein* an early robot story? Discussions of science fiction characteristically begin with definitions, and this seems so commonsensical, so natural a procedure, that it requires no explanation. Nevertheless, it is worth noting that discussions of other genres – detective fiction, westerns, or, for that matter, pastorals or revenge tragedies – do not so consistently begin with definitions. In those cases readers

1

and writers seem fairly confident of the boundaries of the genre in question. Perhaps this is so because those genres seem to be defined by their subject matter; detective stories are about crime, westerns are about cowboys, Indians, and life on the old frontier. In what sense is science fiction about science? Even if we accept such topics as time travel or telepathic communication as scientific, how are we to distinguish science fiction from other fiction on grounds of subject matter alone? *Tess of the D'Urbervilles* is as much concerned with the social impact of scientific and technological developments as any science-fiction novel. Is *Airport* science fiction? What about medical novels?

Science fiction is problematic in other ways as well. Most popular literature is formulaic; science fiction is not, at least not in the same way. The crime, the perpetrator, the investigator: the plot formula of detective fiction is capable of marvelous variation, but it is always recognizable as the constant factor of the form. There is no comparably explicit formula to which one can readily point as characteristic of science fiction. Rather, there is a fairly large vocabulary of simultaneously available formulas from which a science-fiction writer can choose, a situation comparable to that of, say, the English popular drama in Shakespeare's day. The alien-encounter story (the alien may be malevolent, benevolent, or neither); the time-travel story; the fable of the questing scientist, mad or otherwise; the dystopian satire; the postapocalypse story; the evolutionary fable — each of these is a recognizable science-fiction category with its own formulaic characteristics, and there are many other categories as

2

well. Western stories, too, employ a variety of plots,
but westerns are readily definable in terms of the symbolic landscape, the peripheral region midway between
civilization and wilderness, in which the action is always set. The settings of science-fiction stories, however, range even more widely than the plots. They may
be as commonplace as contemporary New York or as
exotic as the vicinity of a neutron star. Indeed, there is
some question of whether science fiction is a popular
genre analogous to detective fiction or to westerns.
Edgar Rice Burroughs is a popular writer, but is Olaf
Stapledon?

   If there is a constant factor in science fiction – and
not even this factor will hold if, for example, "The
Heat Death of the Universe" is admitted to the genre –
it is that science-fiction stories either portray a world
that is in some respect different from our own, as for
instance in stories set in the future or on other planets,
or, alternatively, they describe the impact of some
strange element upon our world, as in alien-invasion
stories or evolutionary fables. Science-fiction stories, in
other words, always contain an element of the fantastic. Recognizing this raises the question of how science
fiction is to be distinguished from fantasy, and this is
of course precisely the issue upon which most definitions of the genre focus as well as the point at which
they founder. Generally speaking, these will emphasize
the "realism" of science fiction, its "respect for fact" as
opposed to the "self-indulgence" of fantasy. Robert
Heinlein, for example, defines science fiction as "realistic speculation about possible future events, based solidly on adequate knowledge of the real world, past

and present, and on a thorough understanding of the nature and significance of the scientific method."[1] "Realistic," "solidly," "a thorough understanding" – Heinlein's definition begs many questions. Moreover, it excludes some of his own best work.

Zoline's "The Heat Death of the Universe" makes apparent some of the limitations of approaching science fiction – or, for that matter, any genre – by way of definitions. Zoline's story, if only by virtue of its place of publication, asks to be read in the context of science-fiction expectations. Whether or not it "is" science fiction is finally as much beside the point as whether Marcel Duchamp's signed shovel is art. Sterile arguments over classification are the sort of activity that has given genre criticism a bad name. A literary genre is not a pigeonhole but a context for writing and reading – or, in Claudio Guillén's suggestive phrase, "an invitation to form."[2] Instead of thinking of science fiction as a thing, a kind of object to be described, it is perhaps more useful to think of it as a tradition, a developing complex of themes, attitudes, and formal strategies that, taken together, constitute a general set of expectations.

Genres are historical phenomena: they are born, develop, and ultimately contribute to the birth of other genres into which they disappear. Moreover, their origins are wedded to complex cultural, historical, and literary circumstances.

When does science fiction begin? It used to be common for historical surveys to trace science fiction back through the traditions of the fabulous voyage and utopia to the Greeks. Plato has been claimed for science fiction, sometimes on the basis of the Atlantis myth and sometimes on the basis of *The Republic* as a utopia, but Lucian's *True History*, which contains a satiric account of a moon voyage and an interplanetary war, is the progenitor most often cited. Histories of science fiction nearly always mention such early moon voyages as Kepler's *Somnium* (1634), Bishop Godwin's *The Man in the Moon* (1638), and Cyrano de Bergerac's *Voyage dans la lune* (1657), as well as *Gulliver's Travels* (1726) and Voltaire's *Micromégas* (1752). At present Mary Shelley's *Frankenstein* (1818) seems to be widely accepted as the "first real science fiction novel," and the received canon of early works includes stories by Hawthorne and Poe.[3] All these texts bear some resemblance, usually thematic, to science fiction. Nevertheless, from a historical point of view it may be misleading to speak of even such relatively recent figures as Shelley, Hawthorne, and Poe as science-fiction writers. They were clearly important in the formation of the genre — Poe, for example, was a major influence on Verne — but we should understand that in labeling, say, *Frankenstein* as science fiction we are retroactively recomposing that text under the influence of a generic idea that did not come into being until well after it was written.

Conceiving genre as a social phenomenon, as a set of expectations rather than as something that resides within a text, we are on firmest ground if we speak somewhat vaguely about beginnings. We can, however, note that it is in the latter third of the nineteenth century that some sense of the "scientific romance" as a distinct genre begins to emerge. There was a marked increase in the volume of science-fictional activity in this period. Verne's *From the Earth to the Moon* (1865) and *Round the Moon* (1870) began a vogue for "realistic" interplanetary voyages, first to the moon and then, in the 1880s and 1890s when Schiaparelli's *canali* were in the news, to Mars. G. T. Chesney's *The Battle of Dorking* (1871), a monitory fiction of Germany conquering England that was prompted by the Franco-Prussian War, initiated an interest in future war tales, and Edward Bellamy's *Looking Backward* (1888) began a wave of speculative fiction concerned with future societies. By the end of the century we find that a new literary form is being acknowledged. In 1898, for example, a reviewer of *The War of the Worlds*, citing Verne and Stanley Waterloo's *The Story of Ab* (1897), notes that Wells's novel belongs to a new literary kind:

Following in the wake of the sciences for half a century is a new species of literary work, which may be called the quasi-scientific novel. From M. Verne's prophetic submarine boat to Mr. Waterloo's prehistoric caveman, one could classify a score of romances which try to put into imaginative form the latest results in science and mechanics. Like all literature, too, the new novel is not content with presenting living embodiments of the truth, but is fain to make guesses at the future. It is as yet experimental, and is quite too young to have produced an enduring masterpiece.[4]

Verne and Wells were of course the most prominent figures in establishing a sense of the scientific romance as genre. Between them they created a mental location for the form so that later writers were able to think of themselves as working in an identifiable tradition.

Genres are born from other genres.[5] They come into being when individual writers adapt earlier forms in response to new circumstances. An extended discussion of the milieu in which science fiction came into being is not necessary here, but it would include a history of the crisis of religious faith in the nineteenth century, a discussion of the idea of progress, a consideration of the remarkable technological developments of the latter half of the century, and an account both of nineteenth-century science and of the growth of popular interest in science. In any case, as the original name "scientific romance" suggests, science fiction is perhaps most fruitfully regarded as a transformation of earlier forms of romance. An analysis of, say, Wells's *The Time Machine* (1895) along these lines might indicate how that text involves not only an inversion of the utopian romance – the time traveler expects to find a future more advanced than the present – but also a displacement of the gothic pattern of sin and retribution. In gothic novels the crime is usually an individual act. Here the crime is social, the repression and dehumanization of the working classes, an ancient sin that is gradually revealed in an epiphany of horror as the traveler discovers the true nature of the relations between the Morlocks and the Eloi. Moreover, the book as a whole is a displaced fabulous voyage with time substituted for the usual medium of space, and the narrative follows the pattern of a quest romance – the object of the quest is the truth about the future – moving, like many quest romances, toward a final, apocalyptic moment of revelation in which the transcendent and the mundane interpenetrate as the traveler witnesses the fate of life on earth.

Understanding that science fiction is a version of romance is perhaps the necessary prerequisite to discussion of the genre. We do not expect romances to provide psychological portraits or fully rendered images of the world as we know it. Rather, we expect to hear of marvels and adventures in strange places populated in some romance genres by such preternatural creatures as giants and dragons. From the beginning, characters in science fiction have tended to be types rather than personalities — the scientist, the ordinary man, the religious fanatic — and equivalents to the exotic settings of other forms of romance have been found under the sea or on the moon. Most commonly, science fiction achieves the distancing of romance by setting its narratives in the future. In realistic fiction, setting tends to be primarily a context for character; in romance forms, setting typically receives much more emphasis. Indeed, sometimes the setting of a romance will be more alive, will have more personality, than any of the characters. In *The Faerie Queene*, for instance, the most memorable and often the most dramatic parts of the poem tend to be the descriptions of such crucial locales as Lucifera's palace in Book I or the Garden of Adonis in Book III. In science fiction, too, the most active element in the story is frequently neither character nor plot but landscape.

Wizards and magicians — Spenser's Archimago or Shakespeare's Prospero — are common in early forms of romance. In later romance genres such as the gothic novel, we find displaced versions of the wizard in such daemonically possessed figures as Father Ambrosio in *The Monk*. Indeed, at the core of all romance forms appears to be a Manichaean vision of the universe as a struggle between good and bad magic. Science fiction has its own rationalized versions of the romance wizard. Wells's time traveler is early on in the tale accused of being a parlor magician. What the story demonstrates is that the traveler is not a charlatan but a genuine mage. Time machines, rocket ships, and other technological wonders – all signs of the power of science – generally, but not always, function in science fiction as equivalents to white magic. Science is usually opposed by nature, and the narrative of science-fiction stories typically involves a struggle between mystified versions of science and nature conceived as ultimate antagonists – as they are in *The Time Machine*, which can be analyzed as a progressive revelation that the bad magic of nature, entropy, is finally more powerful than man.[6]

One advantage of a historical approach to science fiction is that it allows us to understand the literary logic of the genre as it has developed. A fairly clear series of periods can be distinguished: the early phase from 1870 to about 1910, principally associated with Verne and Wells; the efflorescence of popular writing in the following twenty-five years, associated with such writers as Edgar Rice Burroughs and E. E. Smith and with Hugo Gernsback's founding of the first of the specialty magazines, *Amazing Stories*, in 1926; the "Golden Age" of the 1940s, associated with John W. Campbell's editorship of *Astounding Stories*; the broadening of thematic range in the 1950s, particularly in *Galaxy* and *The Magazine of Fantasy and Science Fiction*; and the period of stylistic and thematic experimentation that began in the 1960s and that is sometimes referred to as the "New Wave." Examined at close hand, the form's development no doubt seems unique, a record of the particular activities of individual writers and editors. In a wider view, however, it becomes evident that science fiction's history shares certain large features with the history of other genres.

Any genre appears to develop in at least two phases. First, by combining and transforming earlier forms, the genre complex assembles and the idea of the genre's existence gradually appears. Later, a generically self-conscious phase occurs, one in which texts are based on the now explicit form. Thus we can distinguish between primary epic such as the *Iliad* and secondary epic such as the *Aeneid*, which depends upon an established sense of the epic genre. Similarly, we can speak of Theocritus' *Idylls* and Virgil's *Eclogues* as representative of primary and secondary phases of pastoral, or of More's *Utopia* and Swift's *Gulliver's Travels* as representative of primary and secondary phases of utopian writing. All texts require generic models, but whereas More creates his text by combining and adapting such earlier forms as the Platonic dialogue and the voyage narrative, later writers have the *Utopia* itself available as a model and point of departure. Wells's *Time Machine*, as I have suggested, can be analyzed as an adaptation of utopian writing. Indeed, the text explicitly evokes the utopian genre when the traveler remarks that he discovered very little about

the practical details of the future world: "In some of
these visions of Utopias and coming times which I
have read, there is a vast amount of detail about
building, and social arrangements, and so forth. But
while such details are easy enough to obtain when the
whole world is contained in one's imagination, they are
altogether inaccessible to a real traveller amid such
realities as I found here."[7] *The Time Machine* represents both a late phase of utopian writing and an early
phase of science fiction.[8]

Thinking now in terms of primary and secondary
phases, it is probably accurate to extend our conception of the genre's formative period into the
1930s — that is, through the work of Zamiatin, Capek,
Stapledon, Huxley, and the early popular writers. C. S.
Lewis' *Out of the Silent Planet*, however, represents an
example of a writer who evokes and manipulates the
expectations of the science-fiction genre itself. Lewis'
protagonist, Ransom, has read science fiction, "H. G.
Wells and others," and he approaches his voyage to
Mars with preconceptions that prove inaccurate:

He had read of "Space": at the back of his thinking for years
had lurked the dismal fancy of the black, cold vacuity, the
utter deadness, which was supposed to separate the worlds.
He had not known how much it affected him till now — now
that the very name "Space" seemed a blasphemous libel for
this empyrean ocean of radiance in which they swam. He
could not call it "dead"; he felt life pouring into him from it
every moment.

Discovering that Mars is inhabited, Ransom naturally
expects the Martians to be like the monsters of his

reading, "insect-like, vermiculate or crustacean" horrors of "superhuman intelligence and insatiable cruelty," and, naturally, they turn out to be quite different.[9]

Out of the Silent Planet appeared in 1938, the same year in which John W. Campbell became editor of *Astounding Stories*. It is usual to identify Campbell's editorship as a crucial moment in the genre's development and to speak of how Campbell improved the quality of writing in the science-fiction magazines by insisting upon serious and intelligent stories and by cultivating such new writers as Isaac Asimov, Robert Heinlein, and Theodore Sturgeon. Significantly, Campbell's writers, like Campbell himself, were second-generation authors: they had all read widely in earlier science fiction from Verne and Wells to Burroughs and E. E. Smith, and they were concerned with reforming an already established genre. It is in Campbell's *Astounding* that we begin to find popular science fiction moving emphatically into a secondary and self-conscious phase.

Asimov's "Foundation," for example, which first appeared in *Astounding* in 1942, can be read as an attempt to reshape such earlier popular writing as that of E. E. Smith. Mighty spaceships contending in gargantuan cosmic battles — this sort of material had become commonplace in the 1930s in stories that were celebrations of brute physical power on the largest imaginable scale. "Foundation," too, is gigantic in scale: the narrative is set against a background of a declining galactic empire that is beginning to lose control of peripheral regions, an empire conceived on the model of the popular conception of Rome in its decline. But instead of physical power Asimov's story celebrates intelligent independence of mind, describing how through clever political manipulation a small but sophisticated world, Terminus, can avoid being overwhelmed by its much more powerful neighbor, Anacreon. "Foundation" implicitly evokes the kind of "action-packed" science fiction that it is rejecting when Anselm Haut Rodric, the Anacreontic envoy to Terminus, speaks during dinner of his exploits in battle, telling a tale of "mangled spaceships" in "minute technical detail and with incredible zest."[10] Salvor Hardin, on the other hand, the embodiment of the story's positive values, has as his motto, "Violence is the last refuge of the incompetent." Violence versus intelligence: the story suggests an analogy between the Terminus–Anacreon relationship and that of Asimov himself to earlier writers. Perhaps, then, it may not be accidental that both the antagonist world, Anacreon, and its representative, Anselm Haut Rodric, bear the names of ancient writers.

The generic self-consciousness of "Foundation" is related to the story's departure from the values of space opera. The generic self-consciousness of *Out of the Silent Planet* is also related to a shift in ideology, one that might be characterized as regressive: Lewis substitutes an older Christian world view for the conventional scientific materialism of the genre and composes his text in the field of literary tension that this substitution creates. Indeed, the movement from primary to secondary texts in a genre is normally associated with some such change in values, which may be referred either to the individual writer or to the cultural context, as, for example, the shift from the heroic individualism of Homer's Achilles to the social piety of Virgil's Aeneas. We should note that, although "Foundation" rejects violence as a source of power, it preserves the concern with power itself, as Virgil preserves the epic's generic concern with heroism. Generic development is rarely if ever a matter of total metamorphosis; continuity is maintained, and thus the allusive interplay between later and earlier texts is made possible.

In science fiction's secondary phase we frequently find witty variations on established themes, stories that are almost wholly dependent upon the reader's previous experience of the genre. As examples one might cite Heinlein's play with the paradoxes of time travel in "By His Bootstraps" (1941) or in "All You Zombies" (1959), in which a time traveler who has undergone a sex-change operation not only encounters both earlier and later versions of himself but turns out to be his own father and mother. Sometimes these stories are explicitly parodic, such as "Surface Tension" (1952), James Blish's tale of an epic journey undertaken by microscopic creatures in a tiny spaceship from one puddle to another. Having crossed space, Blish's creatures encounter a bug-eyed monster and a beautiful girl who inquires whether they are "gods from beyond the sky." Like many secondary texts, "Surface Tension" can be read as an exercise in generic criticism, a comment upon the giganticism of stories that pretend to significance because they are concerned with entire galaxies and other "large" matters. In this phase, too, we find hybrids, self-conscious experiments in mixed forms such as Alfred Bester's science-fiction detective story, *The Demolished Man* (1951), in which the protagonist is a murderer attempting to outwit a telepathic police force.

Because the range of any genre is limited, writers are always in danger of exhausting the form's potential. In late texts such as *Paradise Lost* or *The Prelude* in epic there is characteristically a movement toward interiorization, a strategy that allows for a temporary revitalization of the whole generic field as spiritual or psychological correlatives replace physical action. Science fiction begins as a way of reexteriorizing romance, a way of writing about tangible marvels that need not be allegorized like Spenser's dragons and giants in order to command belief. Nevertheless, even as early as the Golden Age we can perhaps see the process of interiorization beginning in Asimov's substitution of intellectual for physical power or in the increasing interest in stories concerned with supernormal mental powers following A. E. van Vogt's *Slan* (1940). The process is more marked, however, in somewhat later narratives such as Blish's "Common Time" (1953), which deals with temporal dislocations of faster-than-light travel, or in Daniel Keyes's "Flowers for Algernon" (1959), which presents in diary form the story of a moron who undergoes a temporarily successful experiment in intelligence enhancement.

Interiorization typically involves treating the material of a genre as metaphor rather than literal fact, as Milton, say, treats epic warfare in *Paradise Lost*. Ray Bradbury is one of the earliest to employ the material of science fiction in this way – nearly any story in *The*

Martian Chronicles (1950) might be cited as an example — and in this he can perhaps be seen as a forerunner of the current period, the New Wave of the 1960s and 1970s. In her introduction to *The Left Hand of Darkness* (1969), Ursula K. Le Guin makes a critical statement that contrasts starkly with Heinlein's definition of science fiction as "realistic speculation about future events" and that nicely suggests the current ethos.

All fiction is metaphor. Science fiction is metaphor. What sets it apart from older forms of fiction seems to be its use of new metaphors, drawn from certain great dominants of our contemporary life — science, all the sciences, and technology, and the relativistic and the historical outlook, among them. Space travel is one of these metaphors; so is an alternative society, an alternative biology; the future is another. The future, in fiction, is a metaphor.[11]

Such writers as Brian Aldiss, J. G. Ballard, Samuel Delany, Philip Dick, and Le Guin are representative of this radical reinterpretation of the genre. In Aldiss' *Cryptozoic* (1967), for example, time travel becomes a mental phenomenon accomplished by taking a drug that subverts normal space-time "prohibitions" built into the brain. Similarly, Dick repeatedly writes what might be called epistemological science fiction, constructing situations in which the point is the impossibility of drawing distinctions between fantasy and reality, as in *Ubik* (1969) in which it gradually becomes apparent that the entire narrative may be the dream of a dead man whose brain has been kept artificially functioning.

    I began this discussion of science fiction as a tradition with Zoline's "The Heat Death of the Universe." Perhaps now we can understand that story not as an isolated curiosity but as an extreme example of the transformation of the generic field into metaphor. Perhaps, too, the kinds of radical displacements and transformations that have appeared in current science fiction should be considered a third phase in the genre's development, one analogous to such radical adaptations of epic as *The Prelude* or *Ulysses*. As Zoline's story suggests particularly well, the generic boundaries become increasingly problematic as the genre's quest for new material leads into this tertiary phase.

It is important now to distinguish between individual texts and the idea of a genre and thus to adopt a quite different approach to the subject. Texts are concrete and particular. Generic ideas are not only more abstract than individual texts; they are fundamentally different in nature. They provide, to employ Fredric Jameson's useful term, the "environment" in which texts are written, the matrix that makes composition possible.[12] Texts define themselves in relation to the available system of genres. They may present themselves as wholly within a given genre — *The Aeneid* defines itself as an epic — or as combinations or other transformations of generic ideas. Thus Sidney's *Arcadia* presents itself as a combination of epic and pastoral, Joyce's *Ulysses* as a metaphorical extension of the novel into epic. Texts are comparable to utterances in a language. Generic ideas are comparable to language itself; they exist as elements within a continuously changing system of mutually defining terms.

In language, as Ferdinand de Saussure has sug-

gested, there are no positive terms, only differences.[13]
This is to say that an element of language has value
only insofar as it differentiates itself from other, con-
trasting elements at the same level. In a similar fashion, genres distinguish themselves from other genres:
comedy asserts that it is not tragedy, the romance
asserts that it is not the novel, and science fiction
asserts that it is not fantasy. I mentioned earlier that
definitions of science fiction typically focus on the line
between science fiction and fantasy. Conceiving
generic ideas as a system analogous to language helps
us to understand why this issue continually recurs: in a
sense, science fiction – or, rather, the idea of science
fiction as a genre – does not exist except insofar as it
differentiates itself from fantasy.

Both science fiction and fantasy of the sort associated with William Morris, Charles Williams, and J. R.
R. Tolkein are modern genres, dependent upon the
prior existence of the realistic novel – the major tradition of fiction from Richardson to Updike – as the
dominant narrative form. The rise of the realistic novel
in the eighteenth century led to a transformation of
the whole system of narrative genres. Modern genres
tend to distinguish themselves according to the kind of
reality represented – historical or contemporary, social
or psychological, public or domestic – and even more
fundamentally according to the relationship of the
story to reality: Is the fiction realistic or fantastic? The
major Renaissance genres, however, tended to form
themselves around the kinds of characters employed – noble or base, knights or shepherds, warriors
or lovers – and the kinds of plots. An early text such as

18

The Faerie Queene thus cannot properly be called "fantasy" because the term has value only in the modern literary system. The appearance of the realistic novel, however, led to a retrospective reevaluation of such narratives as *The Faerie Queene*, which could now be understood as "not realistic" in a new sense. The appearance of the realistic novel thus created a potential space in the literary system for a genre between the old romance and the new novel, one that was neither "realistic" nor "not realistic." The space was filled by the gothic novel. Although in his preface to the second edition of *The Castle of Otranto* Walpole puts the issue in positive rather than negative terms, nevertheless he appears to conceive the matter in something like this fashion. *The Castle of Otranto*, he says,

was an attempt to blend the two kinds of romance, the ancient and the modern. In the former all was imagination and improbability: in the latter, nature is always intended to be, and sometimes has been, copied with success. Invention has not been wanting; but the great resources of fancy have been dammed up, by a strict adherence to common life. But if in the latter species Nature has cramped imagination, she did but take her revenge, having been totally excluded from the old romances . . . The author of the following pages thought it possible to reconcile the two kinds.[1]

Science fiction appeared at about the same time as modern fantasy, and both genres took form against the background of the dogmatic realistic or naturalistic movement of the later nineteenth century. Like the gothic's filling of a space between what Walpole refers to as the "two kinds of romance," science fiction can be seen as filling a space between the opposed forms of the new realism and "pure" fantasy. On the one hand, by portraying a world that is always in some respect fantastic, science fiction differentiates itself from realism; on the other, by invoking the scientific ethos to assert the possibility of the fictional worlds it describes, science fiction differentiates itself from fantasy. At issue in these distinctions is not, of course, the literal possibility or impossibility of the fictional world but, rather, the kind of relationship between the text and the empirical world that the story asks the reader to pretend to be true. If it were possible to walk through walls, a fantasy on this theme would, insofar as it wished to be read as fantasy, require us to pretend that such penetrations were impossible. Science fiction, however, presents its worlds as possible even when they plainly are not. Yielding to the temptation to be epigrammatic, one might describe science fiction as a form of the fantastic that denies it is fantastic.[15]

In the genre's early phase, individual texts often go to great lengths to locate themselves as science fiction. Thus Verne, shooting his men to the moon in a giant gun, innundates us with information about distances, muzzle velocities, and the power of various kinds of explosives. Wells adopts what he called "scientific patter," such as the time traveler's extended analogy between movement in time and movement in space. In later phases, stories launch us without patter into worlds in which time travel, telepathy, and other marvels are possible, depending upon the reader's previous experience with the genre; characteristic themes and motifs become the principal generic signals.

GENRE

The characteristic rhetorical posture of science fiction naturally implies a philosophical position. Realism
presents itself as making a positive statement about
the world: "This is the way it is." Fantasy, which depends upon our understanding that its worlds are impossible, makes a negative statement: "This is the way
it isn't." Indirectly, fantasy affirms the world of realism:
reading a story about elves reinforces the conviction
that elves do not exist in the world. This may help to
explain the appeal that such stories have for children
as games in which their sense of reality is tested and
confirmed. Science fiction, however, challenges our
sense of the stability of reality by insisting upon the
contingency of the present order of things. Indeed,
science fiction not only asserts that things may be different; as a genre it insists that they will and must be
different, that change is the only constant rule and
that the future will not be like the present. One might
call fantasy a conservative form, whereas in principle
science fiction might be called subversive.

Regarded as an ideal form, science fiction's place
in the generic system is clear. It is when we descend to
particular texts that fruitless debates about classification occur. In order to locate the points at which these
debates are most likely to occur, it may be useful now
to conceive the opposition between fantasy and
science fiction in terms of Roman Jakobson's distinction between metaphor and metonymy as poles of literary behavior.[16] The changed worlds of fantasy are
presented as literary substitutions for reality; they are
related to the empirical world paradigmatically or metaphorically, as in Tolkein's substitution of "hobbit" for

"Englishman." The changed worlds of science fiction, however, are presented as logical extensions of reality; they are related to the empirical world syntagmatically or metonymically. This is what is meant when science fiction is called an extrapolative form. No text, however, is constructed purely metaphorically or purely metonymically; both principles are at work in science fiction as in all discourse. Wells, for example, may present time travel as an extrapolation, but the principle behind the idea is metaphorical: time is substituted paradigmatically for space.

Employing Jakobson's terms, we can imagine a spectrum ranging between ideal poles of science-fiction worlds generated by pure metonymy and pure metaphor.[17] *Twenty Thousand Leagues Under the Sea* will fall toward the metonymic end of the spectrum. *The Time Machine* will fall closer to the center. Edgar Rice Burroughs, Bradbury's *Martian Chronicles*, and much recent science fiction such as that of Aldiss and Dick will fall toward the metaphorical end of the spectrum, as indeed will all those texts in which readers tend to find problems distinguishing between science fiction and fantasy. Conceiving science fiction in this manner helps to explain why the genre has become increasingly problematic. Not only has there been a natural tendency in later phases to rely upon the reader's previous experience of science fiction rather than upon more explicit generic signals, but the movement toward internalization and metaphor has inevitably shifted the genre's center away from the metonymic pole.

Genres are limited. Particular genres may exhaust

themselves but, frequently, the corresponding mode, an abstraction from the genre, will survive and will lead to the appearance of new generic forms. The "heroic" survives the epic, the "pastoral" the eclogue. In the nineteenth century the utopian genre yielded a mode that, particularly in the inverted form of the dystopia, contributed to the new genre, science fiction. Evidently genres have souls, and these are capable of transmigration. The movement from the specificity of "genre" to the vague and more generalized status of "mode" is of course gradual and continual and difficult to recognize while it is happening. Nevertheless, the appearance of such radically problematic texts as "The Heat Death of the Universe" perhaps suggests that science fiction's history as a distinct genre may be approaching its end. More fundamentally, the recent shift of the mainstream of narrative fiction away from psychological realism — I am thinking of the work of Barth, Barthelme, Borges, Marquez, and Pynchon — perhaps indicates that the whole system of genres which has defined science fiction as a distinct form may be in flux and that the boundary between science fiction and the mainstream may become increasingly more difficult to recognize.[18]

PARADIGM

What, then, is the "soul" of science fiction? What is the genre's characteristic field of interest? Let us approach this problem by way of a text that has as good a claim as any to being considered archetypal, Wells's classic tale, "The Star" (1897).[1]

In this story a wandering planet enters the solar system. At first the intruder is a remote speck interesting only to astronomers, but then it collides with Neptune and the two planets, fused into a single incandescent mass and clearly visible to the naked eye, plunge toward the sun. Crowds gather to watch the apparition, which grows steadily brighter until it surpasses the moon. By this time it has become evident that the object may collide with the earth. As the fiery intruder approaches, the earth's temperature rises: snows melt, floods and violent storms begin, earthquakes and volcanic eruptions ravage the world. Millions die. Ultimately the earth escapes being struck; nevertheless, the world's temperature has been raised permanently and the remnants of mankind are forced to migrate toward the poles. The story concludes with an abrupt shift in perspective as we are suddenly introduced to Martian astronomers who have followed the cosmic event and are principally surprised at how little affected the earth has been: "All the familiar continental markings and the masses of the seas remain intact." The single change, as far as they can see, is a slight shrinkage of the polar icecaps. "Which only shows," Wells comments, "how small the vastest of human catastrophes may seem, at a distance of a few million miles."

Wells's intruding planet is a logical extrapolation

24

from nineteenth-century astronomy, and it is easy to defend this story in terms of "possibility." Interestingly, however, the possibility of a cosmic intruder is not established, as it might well have been, on the basis of positive astronomical knowledge that such wandering planetary objects may exist. Indeed, Wells exaggerates our ignorance of what he calls the "black mystery" of the heavens, and his strategy for validating his idea is conspicuously indirect. Through the story's title – the cosmic intruder is not, properly speaking, a star – and through such portentous phrases as "overhead . . . blazed the star of coming doom," he evokes astrology, the discredited counterpart of the true science of the heavens. Indirectly, then, Wells implies that his story is true astronomy, a version of baleful stars producing earthly upheaval that might indeed be possible. The procedure is one of implying credibility by invoking the incredible, of asserting that the story is scientific by denying that it is unscientific.

Formally, the narrative is an extended epiphany, and it may be regarded as a transformation of such characteristic romance revelations of the intersection of the human and the superhuman as Redcross' vision of the New Jerusalem in *The Faerie Queene*. As the concluding evocation of the Martian astronomers suggests, the subject is not so much catastrophe as perspective. Wells's strategy is to insert the familiar sphere of mundane concerns – the world of yawning policemen, hurrying workmen, dissipated revelers – into the larger context of stars, planets, and astronomical events. The effect is to render the familiar strange, to make us grasp the contingency of the ordinary world that we generally take for granted. Significantly, the announcement about perturbations of Neptune's orbit with which the story begins occurs "on the first day of the new year," and the description of the steadily increasing brightness of the approaching object is simultaneously a literal description of an astronomical fact and a metaphorical evocation of the dawning of a new consciousness on earth. At the end, the text mentions "the new brotherhood that grew presently among men," suggesting that the object's close approach and the resulting change in mankind's perspective on its place in the cosmos have had social as well as physical consequences.

"The Star" achieves the characteristic science-fiction effect of "estrangement" or "defamiliarization" by recording the transformation of the familiar into an unfamiliar world through the agency of a fantastic intruder.[2] This may be regarded as the simplest as well as one of the most common patterns that science-fiction narratives follow. We encounter it in every stage of the genre's development from *The War of the Worlds* (1898) through Arthur C. Clarke's *Childhood's End* (1953) or Kate Wilhelm's *Where Late the Sweet Birds Sang* (1976). It is the basic formula of such science-fiction horror films as *The Invasion of the Body Snatchers* (1955) and *The Andromeda Strain* (1971). The extraordinary intruder may be an alien creature, a novel and devastating disease, a climatic or ecological change, a technological innovation, or any of a large number of other possibilities. Sometimes the familiar world is either partially or wholly restored at the story's end, and sometimes it is not. The narrative's

emphasis may fall upon the threat of change, the process of change, or the effects of change.

The second major pattern, that in which we are
launched into an unfamiliar world as in *The Time
Machine, When the Sleeper Wakes* (1899), or *The First
Men in The Moon* (1901), can be regarded as a variation of the first. Narratives that follow this pattern will
often take the shape of a quest for an explanation of
how the world transformation came about. This pattern, too, can be found in every stage of the genre's
development from the three Wells novels cited to
Walter M. Miller's *A Canticle for Leibowitz* (1960) or
Philip Dick's *The Man in the High Castle* (1962). The unfamiliar world may be located on another planet, in
another time, in another "dimension" as in alternate-
history stories, or it may be simply the vehicle in which
men are traveling to one of these locales as in Heinlein's "Universe" (1941). The emphasis may fall upon
the process of transformation — the journey, the search
for causes — or upon the transformed world itself.

In science fiction as in other literature, form is
finally inseparable from content. The familiar in relation to the unfamiliar, the ordinary in relation to the
extraordinary, is always, at least at one level of
generalization, the subject of science fiction. This may
be less apparent in the later than in the earlier phases
of the genre. *The Time Machine* begins in the familiar
world of late Victorian England; only after this has
been established as a reference point does the fiction
move to the future world of the Morlocks and the Eloi.
In later phases, after the principle of world transformation as a generic expectation has been established, we

more often find stories that begin well after such a
transformation has occurred, as Heinlein's "Universe"
does, opening with "There's a mutie! Look out!"³ In
these phases, too, the focus is often less upon the
causes of world transformation – indeed, this element
is frequently omitted or provided in the briefest short-
hand – than upon the nature of the unfamiliar world itself. Generally, as in the case of "Universe" or Le
Guin's *The Left Hand of Darkness,* such stories focus
on a metaphorical rather than a causal relationship
between the changed and the familiar worlds – that is,
they are primarily concerned with the ways in which
science-fiction worlds can be used to explore the
nature and limits of our own reality.

Even if the familiar world is nowhere explicitly invoked in a science-fiction story, it is always implicitly
present as the reference point for the narrative. Most
science-fiction stories do, however, provide some form
of "distance marker," some textual element that allows
us to measure the distance between the unfamiliar and
the familiar worlds. In its most primitive form this may
be a speech in which a character or the narrator directly invokes our world, perhaps with a variation on
the formula "back in the twentieth century they believed that . . . " More often the distance marker is
some other sign of the familiar world inserted into the
fantastic world: for example, the museum containing
nineteenth-century matches as well as other ancient
items that Wells's time traveler discovers in the far
future. Sometimes the sign is literary or linguistic. In
Kingsley Amis' alternate-history novel, *The Alteration*
(1976), the characters discuss a recent book by Philip
Dick, *The Man in the High Castle,* but the story that

the characters have read bears little relation to Dick's
novel. Robert Silverberg's *Nightwings* (1969) begins:
"Roum is a city built on seven hills."[4] The linguistic distance between "Roum" and "Rome" indicates the temporal distance between the fantastic world of the story
and our world. Recognizing which city is meant by
"Roum" is an act in which the two worlds are forcibly
yoked in the reader's mind. Distance markers may thus
be understood as moments in which the science-fiction
story provides a textual representation of its own subject, the relationship between the ordinary and the extraordinary worlds.

All forms of fantastic literature — the gothic, the
romantic tale, and modern fantasy as well as science
fiction — are concerned with the relationship between
the ordinary and the extraordinary. We can be more
specific about science fiction's field of interest if, returning to "The Star" as our archetypal story, we recall
that the agency of world transformation is a physical
object, the intruding planet. We should also note that
Wells's characters are not characters at all in the
novelistic sense, but merely such representative figures
as the mourning woman who is unconcerned with the
planet's approach or the professor of mathematics who
calculates that the planet's course will intersect the
earth's. Wells's protagonist is mankind as a collective
entity; his antagonist, similarly abstract, might be described as the physical circumstances of the cosmos in
which mankind attempts to survive. The narrative,
then, can be interpreted as a model of the relationship
between man and nature.

In the first chapter I suggested that science-fiction

stories typically involve a struggle between science and nature. This is particularly clear in "The Star." At one point Wells's mathematician is described as gazing at the approaching planet "as one might look into the eyes of a brave enemy. 'You may kill me,' he said after a silence. 'But I can hold you – and all the universe for that matter – in the grip of this little brain. I would not change. Even now.'" The metaphor of brave warriors locked in mortal combat is a clue to the displaced romance pattern. Two powers are presented as ultimate antagonists: man's power to comprehend and nature's power to destroy. Because the two powers operate in spheres that have no point of juncture – man's in the immaterial or spiritual, nature's in the physical – the test of strength can never finally be resolved. Even if the planet should "kill" the scientist, it cannot change the fact that he can "hold" nature. And yet the powers are not simply equals. Here, as in romance generally, we are being asked to see the spiritual as superior in worth to the physical. Both powers are magical, but mankind's is white.

"The Star" is science fiction in its most direct form. In other narratives we will find displacements and transformations of the tangible confrontation that this story dramatizes. For example, Pamela Zoline's "The Heat Death of the Universe" may represent a borderline case of science fiction in some respects; nevertheless, it adheres closely to the genre's central region of concern. As in "The Star," the antagonist is nature, the entropic will to chaos that is invading Sarah Boyle's life. The protagonist is the human will to order that Boyle herself embodies. In "The Star" no resolution of the struggle is possible. Here, however, the contention is between directly opposed terms — order and disorder — and in the end the inhuman triumphs over the human, the physical over the spiritual, as Sarah Boyle breaks down in exhaustion and begins hurling glasses, dishes, and eggs about her kitchen. "The Heat Death of the Universe" may be regarded as a metaphorical version of the alien-invasion tale. Like someone "taken over" by an inhuman invader — as in *The Invasion of the Body Snatchers* — Sarah Boyle has become the alien, the agent of entropy's spread. The triumph of entropy is not, however, so complete as the narrative alone suggests. Some measure of irresolution, analogous to the irresolution of "The Star," is created by Zoline's formal device of presenting her text in fifty-four conspicuously numbered paragraphs, many bearing titles such as "Cleaning Up the House" or "Time Pieces and Other Measuring Devices." In this way the text draws attention to itself as an ordering system in which entropy, the story's subject, is contained. Wells's mathematician is able to encompass the destructive forces of nature in his brain; Sarah Boyle is unable to resist entropy, but the text itself implicitly asserts the manner in which nature can be defeated.

Both "The Star" and "The Heat Death of the Universe" are concerned with confrontations between the human — represented by science in Wells and by art or the will to order in Zoline — and the nonhuman. These are the fundamental terms in play in both texts — or, putting the statement in somewhat different terms, we may say that both texts are composed within the semantic space created by the opposition of

31

ALIEN ENCOUNTERS

human versus nonhuman. Indeed, this opposition defines the semantic space, the field of interest, within which science fiction as a genre characteristically operates. It constitutes what we may call the genre's paradigm. At the level of theme and motif, science fiction seems bewilderingly diverse, composed of such disparate elements as aliens, time machines, spaceships, robots, and telepaths. If we proceed to a higher level of abstraction, however, we can observe the way the concern with the human in relation to the nonhuman projects itself through four logically related categories, which I shall call space, time, machine, and monster. Recognizing these categories and the forms of science fiction that they produce allows us to locate apparently disparate elements in relation to each other and thus to view the genre as a whole.[5]

Space. In this form the nonhuman is projected "out there," as in "The Star." In the spatial form we not only find alien-encounter stories but also most of the fabulous-voyage tales, journeys beneath the earth or above the earth to the moon, other planets, or other stars. This form is characteristically concerned with physical nature and with extraterrestrial creatures, which often may be understood as animated versions of nature. Logically, the spatial form represents the basic — though by no means necessarily the crudest — version of science fiction.

Time. In this form the nonhuman is not an object or a landscape or a creature but a process that reveals itself in time. Humanity is seen as struggling to survive in an ocean of time. Wells's *Time Machine,* which transforms the fabulous voyage into a new kind of story by substituting time for space, may be taken as archetypal. Stories tend to be set in the future or perhaps in an alternate version of the present, and typically they deal with changes in the human condition wrought by some aspect of time. Such narratives tend to become meditations on the meaning of history.

Machine. In the spatial and the temporal forms, the nonhuman figures as the context in which humanity finds itself. In many stories, however, humanity does not merely encounter the nonhuman but is the agency for the production of the nonhuman. Robot stories, computer stories, and other versions of the man-machine confrontation are in this third form. Machines may of course be intangible as well as tangible, as in the case of the social machines of the dystopias. Incidentally, we may note that whereas most dystopias are felt to be science fiction, most utopias are not. This makes perfect sense. Dystopias are always concerned with the human in conflict with the nonhuman. Utopias, on the other hand, are attempts to portray societies that are, according to the author's lights, more fully human than his own.[6]

Monster. The nonhuman may be located within humanity as well as outside it. Stories in this form generally depend upon a transforming agency that corresponds to one of the three preceding categories: an alien encounter may lead to a metamorphosis of humanity, time may lead to a metamorphosis, or man himself may be the agent of his own metamorphosis, as in postatomic apocalypse stories in which the landscape is dominated by mutants. "Monstrosity" may of course be positive as well as negative; superman stories and evolutionary fables of *homo superior* are positive versions of the mode.

Let me emphasize that these are heuristic categories. Obviously, individual texts may often be considered under more than one heading. Kubrick's and Clarke's *2001: A Space Odyssey*, for example, might be discussed as an alien-contact story (space), an evolutionary fable (time), a man-machine encounter (machine), or as a tale of human metamorphosis (monster). These categories must not be conceived as compartments in which to store texts but rather as concepts that are valid insofar as they allow us to analyze the internal thematic structure of the genre.

Recognizing the paradigmatic concern with the human in relation to the nonhuman illuminates science fiction in a variety of ways. For one, it helps us to see how the genre's semantic field is differentiated from that of the dominant tradition of fiction. Naturally there is some overlap. The mainstream of fiction has been sporadically concerned with the natural world as a form of the nonhuman; such texts as *Robinson Crusoe* and *Moby Dick* come immediately to mind, as well as the prominent American tradition of novels set against the background of the forest or the wilderness. We can observe, too, that when the novel turns toward social satire, a concern with social institutions as forms of the nonhuman tends to emerge, as in *Bleak House*. Nevertheless, the novelistic tradition has been centered upon human beings in relation to each other, not upon the human in relation to the nonhuman. This helps to explain why the novel has tended toward individuated characters and why, in its later phases, the movement toward internalization has taken the form of psychological exploration. In science fiction, characters tend to represent aspects of the abstraction "human," and the movement toward internalization here has primarily taken the form of philosophical — particularly epistemological — exploration.

As any list of early writers from Homer and the Greek tragedians through Dante, Spenser, Shakespeare, and Milton suggests, the dominant modern tradition represents a narrowing of the literary field. This may be explained in part as a function of humanists' sense of alienation from the nonhuman world as it has been revealed by science. What, finally, do the laws of physics have to do with us? Or, to put the question in a form that was familiar a few years ago, why go to the moon when there is poverty down here? In any case, it may not be inaccurate to say that, generally speaking, the dominant literary culture since the Renaissance has tended to dismiss the sphere of the nonhuman as irrelevant or uninteresting.

The major exception to this generalization is the romantic movement of the late eighteenth and early nineteenth centuries and its dialogue with nature. It is no accident that such names as Mary Shelley and Edgar Allan Poe arise so frequently in discussions of science fiction, for many of the intellectual and artistic roots of the genre lie in romanticism. In both romantic literature and science fiction, characteristic concerns find expression through strategies of estrangement or defamiliarization; to this end romantic writers generally either employed exotic material — "Kubla Khan" or

"La Belle Dame sans Merci" – or, in the manner of Wordsworth, sought a style "whereby ordinary things should be presented to the mind in an unusual aspect." Moreover, the romantic concern with nature logically led to an interest in science, and thus to such statements as this one of Wordsworth's which clearly looks forward to science fiction:

If the labors of men of science should ever create any material revolution, direct or indirect, in our condition, and in the impressions which we habitually receive, the poet will sleep then no more than at present, but he will be ready to follow the steps of the man of science, not only in those general indirect effects, but he will be at his side, carrying sensation into the midst of the objects of the science itself. The remotest discoveries of the chemist, the botanist, or mineralogist, will be as proper objects of the poet's art as any upon which it can be employed. ("Preface" to *Lyrical Ballads,* 1802)

"Carrying sensation into the midst of the objects of the science itself" – this is indeed one way in which science fiction frequently operates, attempting to convey the taste, the feel, the human meaning of scientific discoveries.

In science fiction the nonhuman is often some aspect of the natural world as revealed by science: for example, the macroscopic world of planets, stars, and interstellar spaces or the microscopic world of the interior of the human body as in the film *Fantastic Voyage* (1966). In its simplest form the nonhuman is presented as a landscape, for instance, the subterranean landscape of Verne's *Journey to the Centre of the*

Earth (1864). Thus the crucial relationship in a science-fiction narrative will often be between the human figures and the landscape, even though the writer may superimpose upon this central relationship other, more conventional, narrative materials such as a love story or a contention between human characters. This natural world may be regarded positively, perhaps as the embodiment of a strange or awesome beauty. Historically, however, science fiction is in large part a response to the cultural shock created by the discovery of humanity's marginal position in the cosmos; therefore we need hardly be surprised to find that more often in science fiction nature is regarded as fundamentally inhospitable to man. This is clearly the attitude both in "The Star" and in "The Heat Death of the Universe," and it is common in stories at all levels of accomplishment from E. E. Smith's naive power fantasies to Le Guin's *The Left Hand of Darkness*. Nevertheless, for some purposes we may consider it irrelevant whether the nonhuman is regarded positively or negatively; structurally, the science-fiction dialogue with the nonhuman may perhaps be seen as an extension of the romantic dialogue with nature.

Still, the human versus nonhuman opposition does not always correspond to the romantic opposition between man and nature. Stories in the spatial and temporal categories will often identify the nonhuman with some aspect of nature. But stories in the machine and, sometimes, in the monster categories often identify the human with the natural. In dystopias, for example, the artificial social world, identified as nonhuman and negatively presented, is generally opposed to nature,

37

which here becomes synonymous with "truly human."
We can clarify this situation by noting that the
paradigmatic opposition of science fiction generally in-
tersects with a secondary opposition between science
and nature. This is easiest to conceive in the form of a
diagram:

Sometimes, as in "The Star," science fiction joins
science and human as allied concepts in confrontation
with nature and nonhuman. Alternatively, as in
dystopias, science fiction joins nature and human in
confrontation with science and nonhuman. The
science-fiction paradigm, in other words, cannot simply
be regarded as a version of romanticism; science fiction, which is concerned with science in a way that
romanticism as such generally is not, represents an independent semantic system.

As the dystopias suggest, science fiction may cast
science solely in the role of the nonhuman. Ray Bradbury's stories often operate this way, opposing the
natural and organic to the mechanical and scientific.
More frequently, however, science figures on both
sides of the human versus nonhuman opposition. This
is clear in "The Star" in which the nonhuman element,
the intruding planet, is a synecdoche for the universe
discovered by astronomy and, by extension, for the
world of science in all its aspects. But science in

another sense also provides the instrument through which Wells's mathematician holds the universe in his brain. In Asimov's *Foundation* series, the nonhuman is the entropic principle operating in time to reduce the galactic empire to barbarism. The human instrument for contending with entropy is the science of "psycho-history" that Hari Seldon has developed in order to manipulate the laws of history and secure the most beneficial possible outcome for mankind. Science, we may say, is often both humanity's magic and its magical opponent.

I have mentioned that science fiction invokes the scientific ethos in order to differentiate itself from other forms of the fantastic. Now we see that science, both as good and as bad magic, also enters science fiction's semantic field. Science is a form of knowledge, and thus we often find an opposition between science and some form of ignorance. In *The War of the Worlds,* for instance, Wells's narrator is paired with a curate who insists upon dealing with the Martian invasion in religious terms: "Why are these things permitted?" he characteristically asks. "What sins have we done?"[7] Eventually the curate goes mad — his religious conceptual framework is simply inadequate to comprehend the truth of the situation — and the narrator is forced to strike him over the head to preserve his own life. The curate's fate is the text's way of categorically rejecting superstition and thus affirming a scientific view of the situation: the Martian invasion has nothing whatsoever to do with humanity's virtues or vices.

The term opposed to science may be "politics,"

"business," "the academy," "the military," or any of a large number of other possibilities, depending on the purposes and ideology of the individual author. The most common contrary, however, is "religion," as in *The War of the Worlds,* and this has general structural significance. Like science fiction, religion is concerned with the relationship between the human and the nonhuman – or, more specifically, with the relationship between between the human and the divine. It should not be surprising, then, to note that whereas in literary form science fiction may be understood as a displacement of romance, in content it may be understood as a displacement of religion.

Kubrick's and Clarke's *2001: A Space Odyssey* (1968) may be understood as primarily about the relations between humanity and the mysterious slabs. As simple geometrical forms, the slabs are opposed both to the film's organic images – the opening primeval land-scape, for instance – and to its images of human machines. Indeed, the most we can say about the slabs is that they are neither natural nor human: in their simplicity they are finally unknowable. Defining man as an aggressive, tool-using animal – juxtapositions and visual echoes establish the spaceships and other machines as extensions of the primeval bone – the film projects the history of humanity as the result of periodic interventions by the slabs. The opening shows man's creation; the middle, focusing on man's uneasy relations with his machines and with himself, suggests both his powers and his limitations; the conclusion, dwelling upon death and rebirth, shows the end of man, his transformation into something nonhuman. The film as a whole can be read as a series of images — the apes, the machines, the slabs, the embryonic starchild floating in space — that constitute an eschatological fable. The slabs, of course, in their unknowable mystery, point to a transcendent power that can best be described as divine.

As in *2001,* the nonhuman in science fiction may be conceived positively, in which case the human is likely to be conceived as fallen and in need of salvation. In its crudest form this pattern appears in those narratives in which extraterrestrials arrive in flying saucers to save humanity from atomic self-destruction. Such stories characteristically move through death and rebirth toward new visions of heaven. Alternatively, the nonhuman may be conceived negatively as a form of the diabolic in dystopias and some alien-invasion stories such as "The Star" or *The War of the Worlds.* In this case the human is likely to be regarded as superior in worth to the nonhuman. Such narratives are characteristically concerned with diabolic enthrallment or with visions of landscapes that may be described as versions of hell.

It is because the content of the genre is a displacement of religion that science-fiction stories are often concerned to disassociate themselves from religion by characterizing it as the ignorant or feeble opposite of science. In Asimov's "Nightfall" (1941), for instance, the displaced religious content is particularly obvious. The story is set on a planet that is part of a multiple star system with the result that darkness falls only once every 2049 years. When night does fall and the hundreds of thousands of stars of the globular cluster in which the system is located are directly seen, the result is madness and civilization's collapse. The climactic appearance of the stars, functioning as the sign of transcendent power, is presented in quasi-religious language as a moment in which horror at the "awful indifference" of the heavens combines with astonishment at their "awful splendor." If mankind could perceive nature directly, it would go mad. Interestingly, Asimov's plot centers on a violent conflict between a group of scientists attempting to study the phenomenon of darkness and a party of religious fanatics who regard the scientists' studies as sacrilege. Precisely because the religious content is so explicit, the text presents itself as a refutation of religion.

Stories in which conflicts between science and religion are superimposed upon the primary opposition between the human and the nonhuman are especially common in science fiction of the Golden Age. Heinlein's "Universe," for example, is structurally like "Nightfall." "Universe" takes place on a vast starship gone astray. Generations have passed since the starship's launching, and the benighted descendants of the original crew have come to believe that their ship is the universe and that such notions as the "Trip" are to be understood in a religious sense. The story concerns the hero's separation from his ignorant society and his educative journey with the aid of an outlaw band of mutants to the long-forgotten "Main Control Room" where he discovers the stars and recognizes that the universe is vaster than anyone has supposed. Once again, a vision of the stars as a sign of the transcendent is at the center of the story, and once again the plot takes the form of a violent conflict between groups representing science and religion, although here the high priests of the religious society are ironically called "scientists."

Texts such as "Nightfall" and "Universe" provide the point of departure for stories such as Arthur C. Clarke's "The Nine Billion Names of God" (1953), which reverse the usual identification of religion with ignorance and thus render the genre's content overt. In Clarke's story a Tibetan monastic order employs the services of a group of computer specialists to complete their centuries-old task of compiling a list of all the possible names of God. The monks believe that, when the list is complete, mankind's purpose will be fulfilled and the universe will end. On the evening that the computer finishes its task, the skeptical scientists look up at the sky: "Overhead, without any fuss," the story concludes, "the stars were going out."[8] It is striking that Clarke places at the center of his story the same sign that Asimov and Heinlein place at the center of theirs. Here, however, the stars signify the false rather than the true world, and — like other signs of false worlds in romance: Spenser's snowy Florimell or the masque of Ceres in *The Tempest* — at the climax they disappear.

Probably most readers would agree that "The Nine Billion Names of God" is limited by a certain facileness. Can Clarke really mean what his story seems to say? This feeling of insincerity is a function of the text's relationship to the normal ideology of science fiction. From Verne and Wells to the present, science fiction has typically asserted a materialistic rather than a spiritualistic point of view; in science fiction the real world is the tangible world of things. This ideology is frequently located in the science–religion opposition: religion is ignorant because the world it imagines is not real. Simply to reverse the expected polarity of the science–religion opposition while maintaining the structure itself intact, as Clarke does, results in a momentary surprise but not in a sense of "seriousness." Everything in the story's structure disconfirms the surprise of the ending.

Recognizing the nature of the problem in Clarke's story exposes the contradiction at the heart of science fiction as a genre. There is an unresolvable incompatibility between science fiction's materialistic ideology and its status as a romance form concerned with essentially religious material and committed to a vision of the world as a conflict between good and bad magic. This contradiction is not necessarily a disadvantage. In fact, the contradiction itself may be understood as the well of the genre's power, and it would be easy to analyze such texts as "The Star," "Nightfall," or "Universe" to demonstrate how they draw vitality from precisely this source.[9]

As Alfred North Whitehead, among others, points out, a tension between spiritualistic and materialistic world views is fundamental in modern culture.[10] Oversimplifying, we might say that modern culture wishes to believe both in the priority of spirit and in the priority of matter, both in free will and in determinism. In the nineteenth century this tension generally took the form of fierce debates between the proponents of science, particularly evolution, and the proponents of religion and the dignity of man. At present we more often encounter the tension in displaced form, in, for example, the antipathy between humanistic and behavioristic psychology. (Interestingly, Freudian psychology, which in the early part of this century seems to have figured as another in the series of deterministic threats to human dignity, now appears to have crossed the semantic boundary and to figure as spiritualistic in opposition to properly "scientific" psychological therapies. Psychoanalysis is regularly accused of being a religion rather than a science.) On the plane of popular culture, the tension is evident in recurrent waves of interest in such pseudo-sciences as astrology and parapsychology and in oriental mysticism. Moreover, in periods of social stress such as the 1960s in the United States, this tension is likely to become particularly evident as dissenters from the predominantly pragmatic and materialistic culture express their position by aligning themselves with various spiritualistic movements. Not surprisingly, dissent from the Vietnam war often manifested itself in such quasi-religious forms as "bearing witness."

As a genre, then, science fiction operates within the space of a basic contradiction in modern culture. Indeed, one of science fiction's principal cultural functions appears to be to produce narratives that mediate between spiritualistic and materialistic world views. Frequently, as in "The Star," the materialistic world view is presented through the spiritualizing categories of romance, in which case the text will retain the contradiction in a more or less disguised form. This formula is characteristic of "hard core" science fiction.

Asimov's *Foundation* series, for example, asserts both a deterministic view of history and a spiritualistic belief in the efficacy of individual free will. Historical forces are conceived as analogous to classical physical forces: at various points the laws of motion and of the behavior of gases are invoked to explain the historical process. The narratives, however, repeatedly celebrate the intelligent and independent actions of an individual — Hari Seldon, Salvor Hardin, Hober Mallow — who triumphs over his opponents by coming to understand the nature of history. Curiously, the way the hero typically reveals his capacity for bold independence is by doing nothing.

Alternatively, instead of suppressing the incompatibility of the spiritualistic and the materialistic world views, a text may focus directly upon the contradiction, questioning its validity. Such narratives generally take the form of a progressive discovery of the interpenetration, or even of the identity, of matter and spirit. Olaf Stapledon's novels characteristically operate this way, dissolving normal categories of thought. At one point in *Last and First Men* (1930), the moon's orbit is found to be decaying faster than physical theory alone would predict, and the narrator explains that men had not yet discovered "the connexion between a planet's gravitation and its cultural development."[11] C. S. Lewis' *Out of the Silent Planet,* Walter M. Miller's *A Canticle for Leibowitz,* and many of the texts produced by the current metaphorizing and internalizing phase of the genre operate in a similar fashion. What is the difference between matter and spirit in a world such as that of Brian Aldiss' *Cryp-*

tozoic where one can travel in time by taking a mind-altering drug?

Understanding science fiction's role as a mediator between the spiritual and the material helps to explain the genre's interest in such quasi-scientific topics as telepathy, teleportation, telekinesis, faster-than-light travel, matter transmission (which may be understood as a mechanized version of teleportation), and time travel. It also helps to explain the genre's interest in artificial life forms, mechanical spirits such as robots, androids, intelligent computers, and cyborgs. (Computer psychiatrists have become a popular motif in current science fiction.) All of these topics can be interpreted as points at which the spiritual and the material intersect. Moreover, understanding science fiction's role in this way helps to illuminate further why Clarke's "The Nine Billion Names of God" seems so facile. Rather than mediating between the spiritual and the material, this story finally rejects the physical world. At the opposite end of the spectrum is the kind of text that is sometimes associated with Hugo Gernsback's editorship of *Amazing Stories* in which a flimsy narrative provides the excuse for a popular exposition of some technological or scientific point. Here, too, there is little mediation, and these stories also seem finally trivial.

Science fiction's role as mediator between the spiritual and the material is in alignment with its role as mediator between the human and the nonhuman. Generally speaking, the spiritual may be identified as the human, the realm of meaning that is opposed to the meaningless realm of the nonhuman. An atom, a star, or a galaxy in itself means nothing; it is, in every sense of the word, insignificant. The nonhuman acquires significance only when it is brought into relationship with the human. And when this happens the human versus nonhuman opposition is inevitably subverted: the nonhuman becomes part of human experience. Something like this is perhaps what Wordsworth had in mind when he spoke of the poet "carrying sensation into the midst of the objects of the science itself." The passage I quoted earlier from the "Preface" to *Lyrical Ballads* continues:

The remotest discoveries of the chemist, the botanist, or mineralogist, will be as proper objects of the poet's art as any upon which it can be employed, if the time should ever come when these things shall be familiar to us, and the relations under which they are contemplated by the followers of these respective sciences shall be manifestly and palpably material to us as enjoying and suffering beings. If the time should ever come when what is now called science, thus familiarized to men, shall be ready to put on, as it were, a form of flesh and blood, the poet will lend his divine spirit to aid the transfiguration, and will welcome the being thus produced, as a dear and genuine inmate of the household of man.

The transfiguration of the world of science is, of course, exactly what happens in science fiction as men are brought into dialogue with alien creatures or as human beings explore the microscopic or macroscopic worlds that science has revealed. Inevitably, the notion of what constitutes the "household of man" is also changed.

PARADIGM

Science fiction operates, then, not merely by sustaining the human versus nonhuman opposition but by simultaneously and continuously subverting it, generating fables that transfigure both the idea of the nonhuman and the idea of the human. The space that the genre inhabits is not a prison, rigid and unyielding, but a flexible and dynamic field of semantic tension. It is this condition that makes a living genre possible.

SPACE

Concerned with the human in relation to the nonhuman, science fiction could only emerge in the context of a culture that articulates crucial aspects of its experience in those terms. Moreover, because it represents a secular transformation of religious concerns, science fiction could only emerge in a context in which the claims of traditional religion were still felt but in which belief was at best problematic. A story such as "The Star" with its vision of the vast emptiness of interstellar space is dependent upon a sense of God's withdrawal from the cosmos and upon a radical sense of alienation, of unbridgeable difference between the human and the nonhuman worlds. At one time, we know, this sense of alienation from the natural world did not exist. Then the cosmos itself was a sacrament, a manifestation of immanent diety linked to the human world by love, by the great chain of the plenitude of the created universe, and by the multitude of correspondences between the human and the natural spheres, both participating in the magic of the divine logos. The societies of Dante or of Ariosto or even of Kepler might have their stories of passages through the weightless center of the earth or of journeys to an inhabited moon, but such stories could not be science fiction in the same sense as Wells's fable.

It is commonplace to observe that the seventeenth century is the epoch in which man discovers his isolation from the world of things, the period in which human thought distinguishes itself from nature in order to examine it and in this act disengages itself from the

object of its study.[1] In treating motion mathematically
and thus draining nature of such Aristotelian anthropo-
morphisms as "will" and "desire," Galileo founded
modern science. But the shift from a sacramental to an
alienated sense of the cosmos did not come into being
until long after Galileo. The Copernican revolution in
astronomy is often employed by modern writers as the
symbol of man's displacement from the central position in the world, but the Copernican universe was still
very much a sacramental one, and the revolution was
not at first felt as a demotion of human importance.
For Copernicus himself the solar system was a temple
and the sun a magical sign of God:

In the middle of all sits the Sun on his throne. In this
loveliest of temples, could we place the luminary in any
more appropriate place so that he may light the whole
simultaneously. Rightly is he called the Lamp, the Mind, the
Ruler of the Universe: Hermes Trismegistus entitles him the
God Visible. Sophocles' Electra names him the All-seeing.
Thus does the Sun sit as upon a royal dais ruling his
children the planets which circle about him.[2]

Copernicus' universe was of course finite. The
seventeenth-century comprehension of the infinite void
of cosmic space resulted in a profound philosophical
disorientation. Pascal's vertigo is perhaps the *locus
classicus* for the new sense of infinite immensity – but
Pascal himself is probably not to be simply identified
with this terror of the void, and we should remember
too that the infinite universe as conceived by Newton
was still a cosmos charged with immanent deity, one in
which gravity itself might be understood as the

51

moment-by-moment manifestation of God in the world. "Does it not appear from Phaenomena," Newton wrote in the Queries appended to the Latin translation of his *Optics,* "that there is a Being incorporeal, living, intelligent, omnipresent, who in infinite Space, as it were in his Sensory, sees the things themselves intimately, and thoroughly perceives them, and comprehends them wholly by their immediate presence to himself."[3]

The sense of alienation that informs science fiction is inseparable from the modern scientific world view, but one cannot say simply that the rise of science "caused" the sense of alienation. Indeed, in matters of cultural history the very idea of causation may be misleading. Transformations of culture occur, but not on the model of physical causation, and perhaps the best that the cultural historian can do is to observe the kinds of metamorphoses and reinterpretations of the world that have occurred. In any case, the kind of alienation from the natural world that science fiction presupposes really only comes into being in the nineteenth century, and it is intimately associated with both industrialization and urbanization and with the Victorian crisis of faith, with the disappearance of God that marks the beginning of the modern sense of radical disconnection. Seen from this point of view, the romantic poets' struggle to preserve the connection with nature can be understood as an expression of the moment of separation. Later in the century, however, the melancholy, long, withdrawing roar of the Sea of Faith left exposed the naked shingles of the world, revealing a desert or, worse, a monstrous battleground in which individuals and species fought for survival in a world empty of comfort or meaning. Looking at the universe in the absence of God, the Victorians felt the Pascalian vertigo in a new key. What is human life? "What is it all," Tennyson asked, "but a trouble of ants in the gleam of a million million of suns?"[4]

The Victorian situation of urban man disconnected from God, cut off from nature, separated from other men, is of course our own; it is in the nineteenth century that the modern age of alienation begins. Science fiction can be understood in the context of nineteenth- and twentieth-century spiritual loneliness as a manifestation of our culture's longing to escape the prison-house of the merely human. It might be considered as an attempt to reestablish, in some way that will sustain conviction even in our technological and post-Christian culture, the channels of communication with the nonhuman world. Thus we get the many fables in which through the marvels of science the marvels of the natural world are explored, and thus too the many fables of contact with extraterrestrial beings. It does not matter very much whether the nonhuman is portrayed as diabolic as in "The Star" or as divine as in *2001: A Space Odyssey*. What is important is the attempt to replenish the void, to fill the immense absence with meaning, even if this is accomplished by turning emptiness itself into an antagonist that can be confronted in human terms.

Jules Verne's subject is nature. The *voyages extraordinaires* explore worlds known and unknown: the interior of Africa, the interior of the earth, the deeps of the sea, the deeps of space. Characteristically, Verne's voyagers travel in vehicles that are themselves closed worlds – his imagination projects itself in terms of "inside" and "outside" – from which the immensity of nature can be appreciated in upholstered comfort. The *Nautilus* is the most familiar of these comfortable, mobile worlds; inside all is cozy elegance, the epitome of the civilized and human, while outside the oceans gleam or rage in inhuman beauty or mystery. Roland Barthes finds the principle at the heart of Verne's fictions to be the "ceaseless action of secluding oneself." The known and enclosed space, the comfortable cave, is safe while "outside the storm, that is, the infinite, rages in vain." The basic activity in Verne is the construction of closed and safe spaces, the enslavement and appropriation of nature to make a place for man to live in comfort. "The enjoyment of being enclosed reaches its paroxysm when, from the bosom of this unbroken inwardness, it is possible to watch, through a large window-pane, the outside vagueness of the waters, and thus define, in a single act, the inside by means of its opposite."[5]

Journey to the Centre of the Earth (1864) is just such an exploration of "insideness," except that here the interior world is the nonhuman world, a realm of subterranean galleries, caverns, and seas, and here rather than being the place of enclosed safety the interior world becomes an immensity, a fearful abyss. Abysses dominate the novel. Even before Professor Lidenbrock and his nephew Axel begin their journey into the interior, Axel, the story's narrator, has nightmares in which he finds himself "hurtling into bottomless abysses with the increasing velocity of bodies dropping through space."[6] The idea of the abyss is continually kept before us, and always the danger is as much psychic as physical. Standing on the edge of the first real chasm, Axel speaks of the "fascination of the void" taking hold of him: "I felt my centre of gravity moving, and vertigo rising to my head like intoxication. There is nothing more overwhelming than this attraction of the abyss" (p. 104). The danger, evidently, is of losing one's sense of self and of disappearing, intoxicated, into the infinite void.

The abyss in this novel is a version of the cosmic void, but the geometry of the earthly chasm differs from that of the astronomical infinity, for the earth is round and therefore has both poles and a center. Poles and center are magical loci, the three still places on the turning globe. When the earth is conceived as a bounded world located in unbounded space, the poles are extremities, the furthest points on the globe. Indeed, imagined in this way, the poles are magical precisely because they are the earth's boundaries and thus partake of the numenous power associated with any boundary zone. They are the icy, uninhabitable regions in which human space – the habitable world – meets the nonhuman space of the infinite. To reach and explore the poles is to achieve the completion of the human sphere by defining the earth in its entirety. (This is the meaning that seems to generate the nineteenth- and early twentieth-century obsession with polar exploration.) To reach the center of the globe also means to achieve completion, except that now the earth itself has become the imagined immensity and the attainment of the center means the penetration of the essence, the achievement of the heart of the mystery. The liminal poles are frigid; the mystical center is generally imagined as hot, the fluid, living core of the globe. The earthly chasm thus opens onto a different kind of imaginative space from the astronomical void; at the bottom of the bottomless abyss is the region not of transcendence but of immanence, the locus in which all knowledge, all being, all power are immediately present. To attain the center of the earth, then, means to penetrate the heart of nature, to possess nature absolutely. This is the object of Professor Lidenbrock's and Axel's quest.

Extremes meet and magical opposites are always, in a sense, identical. At the time Verne was writing *Journey to the Centre of the Earth* he was also writing *Captain Hatteras* in which an obsessed adventurer reaches the north pole. The pole itself turns out to be an erupting volcano — magical heat in the center of the regions of cold — and standing on the lip of the polar crater, the margin of the space in which heat and cold, life and death, inside and outside, immanence and transcendence interpenetrate, Hatteras goes mad.[7] Significantly, in *Journey to the Centre of the Earth* Lidenbrock and Axel gain access to the interior by traveling north to the cold and barren arctic limits of the habitable world, Iceland, where they enter the subterranean regions through the cone of the extinct volcano Sneffels.

In traveling to Iceland Lidenbrock and Axel are following the directions given in a runic cryptogram that the professor has discovered in an ancient book: "Descend into the crater of Sneffels Yokul, over which the shadow of Scartaris falls before the kalends of July, bold traveller, and you will reach the centre of the earth. I have done this. Arne Saknussemm" (p. 32). Arne Saknussemm, Lidenbrock knows, was a sixteenth-century Icelandic alchemist. The deciphering of his coded message is the novel's first narrative concern, and this initial action provides the paradigm for the fiction as a whole, for nature itself is conceived here as a kind of cryptogram to be decoded. The key to Saknussemm's message is that it must be read backwards. Likewise, in their descent Lidenbrock and Axel must in effect read nature backwards as they pass through the strata of successively earlier and earlier periods of natural history, eventually finding themselves in a marvelous underground world filled with plants from the era of the giant ferns. Here, too, they discover long extinct animals and in one of the well-known Vernian set pieces witness a mortal battle between a Ichthyosaurus and a Plesiosaurus. Finally, they have a brief glimpse of a giant prehistoric man guarding a herd of mastodons:

Immanis pecoris custos, immanior ipse . . . Yes, indeed, the shepherd was bigger than his flock . . . . He was over twelve feet tall. His head, which was as big as a buffalo's, was half hidden in the tangled growth of his unkempt hair — a positive mane, like that of the primitive elephant. In his hand he was brandishing an enormous bough, a crook worthy of this antediluvian shepherd.   (p. 218)

This journey to the earth's center is thus also a journey into the abyss of evolutionary time, and the fusion of the spatial and temporal modes is one of the novel's sources of power. Temporally projected, the quest for the center, the heart of the mystery, becomes the pursuit of origins, the quest for an ultimate moment of beginning. Understanding this fusion of modes helps to explain why the prehistoric giant is presented in the language of pastoral, a language which activates a literary code of origin that is simultaneously spatial and temporal in mode, both "there" and "then." Understanding this also helps to explain why Lidenbrock's and Axel's journey is presented as a repetition of Arne Saknussemm's journey, as a recovery of an original knowledge once possessed by science in its primeval past. The professor and his nephew in following the mysterious alchemist's footsteps are in effect restoring science to its center and origin.

The process of decoding, of learning to read nature, is in this fiction essentially an action of naming. Like many of Verne's protagonists – think, for instance, of Aronnax and Conseil in *Twenty Thousand Leagues Under the Sea* – Lidenbrock and Axel are obsessive categorizers concerned to find the exact name for each geological stratum, the exact botanical and zoological classification for each underground species of plant or animal. As they descend they are concerned, too, with being able to name their precise position in relation to the surface, the exact number of vertical and lateral feet they have traveled at each point. Moreover, since they are penetrating an unknown world, Lidenbrock and Axel are obliged not only to discover but at times to create names: Hansback for the underground stream that guides them part of their way, Port Gräuben, Axel Island, Cape Saknussemm. The imposition of human names on the nonhuman world is obviously an act of appropriation and conquest, for to be able to decipher and read nature is here to possess it, to drain it of its mysterious otherness and make it part of the human world.

In a characteristic moment Axel describes coming upon a dense subterranean forest composed of weird umbrellalike trees:

I quickened my step, anxious to put a name to these strange objects. Were they outside the 200,000 species of vegetables already known, and had they to be accorded a special place among the lacustrian flora? No; when we arrived under their shade, my surprise turned to admiration. I found myself, in fact, confronted with products of the earth, but on a gigantic scale. My uncle promptly called them by their name.

"It's just a forest of mushrooms," he said.

And he was right. It may be imagined how big these plants which love heat and moisture had grown. I knew that the *Lycopodon giganteum,* according to Bulliard, attains a circumference of eight or nine feet, but here there were white mushrooms thirty or forty feet high, with heads of an equal diameter. There were thousands of them; the light could not manage to penetrate between them, and complete darkness reigned between those domes, crowded together as closely as the rounded roofs of an African city.   (pp. 166-167)

Notice how this passage enacts a conquest, an annexation of alien territory. It begins in tension with Axel unable to name the strange objects. As the passage develops the objects become "just" mushrooms. Next they are associated with the *Lycopodon giganteum* — that is, with a scientific or exact name. Finally they are transformed metaphorically into "the rounded roofs of an African city" so that we are now viewing a primitive but specifically human landscape.

Appropriately, it is Professor Lidenbrock rather

than Axel who in this passage first names the strange objects. From the beginning Lidenbrock is a figure of heroic will engaged in mortal combat with the nonhuman world. Arriving at the base of Sneffels, he is described as "gesticulating as if he were challenging" the volcano. "So that is the giant I am going to defeat!" (p. 85) he announces, in a phrase that sustains this aspect of the fiction. Nothing daunts the professor. Obsessively, he presses forward through every difficulty that lies in the way of the total conquest of nature. "The elements are in league against me!" he cries at a moment when the battle becomes particularly furious: "Air, fire, and water combine to block my way! Well, they are going to find out just how strong-willed I am! I won't give in, I won't move back an inch, and we shall see whether man or Nature will get the upper hand!" (p. 206).

The narrative establishes the professor's significance in part by placing him in opposition to Hans, the phlegmatic Icelandic peasant who acts as guide. By trade an eiderdown hunter, an occupation that significantly involves no struggle with nature since the "hunter" merely collects the feathers from the eider's readily accessible nest, Hans is clever and resourceful but utterly without will. Indeed, Axel calls him "that man of the far West endowed with the fatalistic resignation of the East" (p. 236). The principal thing that Hans cares about is his salary; he insists on having three rix-dollars doled out to him each Saturday evening no matter what the exploring party's situation or location. This mechanical action becomes a comic leitmotif in the novel, but it also suggests the peasant's absolute unconcern about his surroundings, his obliviousness to nature's marvels. Curiously, Hans and Professor Lidenbrock, while in most respects opposed figures, are at one point seen as similar. Sailing across a magnificent underground sea, the professor expresses irritation that they are making no progress toward the center. Axel is delighted with the beautiful views, but Lidenbrock cuts his rapture short:

"I don't give a damn for views. I set myself an object, and I mean to attain it. So don't talk to me about magnificent views . . ."

I took him at his word, and left the Professor to bite his lips with impatience. At six in the evening, Hans claimed his wages, and three rix-dollars were counted out to him. (p.183)

Each imprisoned in his own form of obsession, Lidenbrock and Hans are equally blind to the magic of their surroundings. Paradoxically, the aggressive, passionately involved, Western attitude toward nature can isolate one from nature no less effectively than the passive unconcern of the East.

Both Hans's passivity and Lidenbrock's will to conquer nature are opposed to Axel's romanticism. In a characteristic exchange, the professor and his nephew discuss the fact that the subterranean sea has tides like those on the surface. Axel is amazed and delighted; his uncle, however, finds nothing marvelous in the discovery, pointing out that a subterranean sea will be as subject to the sun and moon's gravitation as any other.

"You are right," I cried. "The tide is beginning to rise."
"Yes, Axel, and judging by the ridges of foam I estimate that the sea will rise about ten feet."

"That's wonderful!"

"No, it's perfectly natural."

"You may say what you like, Uncle, but it all seems extraordinary to me, and I can scarcely believe my eyes. Who would ever have imagined that inside the earth's crust there was a real ocean, with ebbing and flowing tides, winds and storms?" (pp. 170-171)

Axel and his uncle live in different mental universes, Axel embodying the spiritualistic response to the non-human ("That's wonderful!"), Lidenbrock embodying bourgeois materialism ("No, it's perfectly natural."). Not surprisingly, each at various points in the story believes that the other has gone mad.

Near the end of the novel, however, Axel undergoes a conversion. Confronted with what appears to be an insurmountable obstacle to further descent — a huge boulder has sealed the gallery through which they must pass — the youth is suddenly seized by his uncle's daemon of heroic conquest. Now it is Axel who is impatient with delay and who insists that they must immediately blow up the rock with explosive gun-cotton. "The Professor's soul had passed straight into me, and the spirit of discovery inspired me. I forgot the past and scorned the future" (p. 266). Nothing matters for him now except the imperative of penetration to the center. Daemonically possessed, Axel has become, like his uncle, a "hero." His journey has become an initiation into the bourgeois-heroic attitude toward nature, a "going in" in a social as well as a physical sense, and the story ultimately ratifies his new status as an adult male by granting him the hand of the professor's beautiful god-daughter, Gräuben. Nevertheless, as the comic ironies persistently directed against Professor Lidenbrock's limited vision suggest, in the youth's passage something has been lost as well as gained. Caring neither for past nor future, imprisoned in the narrow cage of his own will to dominate, Axel can no longer confront nature except as an antagonist, something utterly apart from himself.

Axel and his uncle never do reach the earth's mysterious center. The gun-cotton explosion triggers a volcanic eruption and, like an animal defending itself against an intrusion into its body, nature expels the explorers, vomits them out along a great volcanic shaft back into the air. Perhaps physical achievement of the center is impossible? Or perhaps reaching that magical locus would mean going mad like Captain Hatteras on the crater of the polar volcano? In any case, the point of furthest penetration, the journey's true climax, is reached, significantly, not by the professor but by his romantic nephew and not in literal reality but in a vision.

Before his conversion, Axel, reflecting upon "the wonderful hypotheses of paleontology," has an extended daydream in which, first, he supposes the subterranean world filling with long extinct creatures: antediluvian tortoises, great early mammals, Pterodactyls and other primeval birds. "The whole of this fossil world came to life again in my imagination." As his dream continues, however, the great animals disappear, the earth grows steadily warmer, and he finds himself in a still earlier age, the period of gigantic vegetation. Even here the dream does not end. Sweeping backward into the abyss of time in quest of the center, the point of origin, Axel finds the heat becoming more and more intense until the earth's granite liquifies and finally the planet itself dissolves into its original white-hot gaseous mass: "In the centre of this nebula, which was fourteen hundred thousand times as large as the globe it would one day form, I was carried through interplanetary space. My body was volatilized in its turn and mingled like an imponderable atom with these vast vapours tracing their flaming orbits through infinity" (pp. 179-180). Climactically, Axel himself disappears, becoming part of the cosmic infinity. At the ecstatic center, the boundary between man and nature, the human and the nonhuman, melts and the explorer merges with the world being explored.

Axel's dream represents, of course, both a romantic alternative to the professor's treatment of nature as an antagonist to be conquered and a fusion of spiritualistic and materialistic world views.[8] Moreover, in Axel's dream, the text calls attention to its own status as a fiction, an imaginary voyage. This kind of fictive self-consciousness was perhaps implicit in such earlier passages as Axel's rhetorical question, "Who would ever have imagined that inside the earth's crust there was a real ocean, with ebbing and flowing tides, winds and storms?" Now, however, in the description of the fossil world coming to life in Axel's imagination – these events are shortly to occur in the narrative proper as the explorers begin to encounter extinct animals and plants – the text's play with its own fictionality is particularly emphatic, and we can hardly miss seeing Axel as momentarily a version of Verne.

SPACE

Expelled from the interior, the explorers emerge in an eruption of Mount Stromboli in Sicily:

We had gone in one volcano and come out by another, and this other was more than three thousand miles from Sneffels, from that barren country of Iceland at the far limits of the inhabited world! The chances of our expedition had carried us into the heart of the most beautiful part of the world! We had exchanged the region of perpetual snow for that of infinite verdure, the gray fog of the icy north for the blue skies of Sicily! (p. 249)

Like the interior, the surface is a realm of infinities, but here the "infinity" is one of welcoming, protective vegetation. Since, in this novel, the interior space has become the void, the exterior world becomes the known and safe space. In reaching Sicily, Lidenbrock and Axel have, ironically, reached the earth's center, the primitive heart not of nature but of the human sphere. "We were in the middle of the Mediterranean," says Axel, "in the heart of the Aeolian archipelago of mythological memory, in that ancient Strongyle where Aeolus kept the winds and storms on a chain" (p. 249). Warm and nourishing in contrast with the icy polar verge, the Sicilian landscape is a paradise of olives, pomegranates, and vines hung with delicious fruit, a landscape that recalls and fulfills the brief evocation of pastoral in the subterranean encounter with primeval man.

With the arrival in Sicily the narrative proper is over; in substituting one code of "centrality" for another, the text has achieved narrative closure. Nevertheless, a further detail remains to be treated in a coda. On the shore of the subterranean sea, after a fierce electrical storm, the explorers' compass seemed to indicate that they had been traveling for nearly 1500 miles in the wrong direction. Had they really been going north when they thought they were going south? The mystery of the compass remains an unexplained phenomenon and a torment to Professor Lidenbrock since "for a scientist an unexplained phenomenon is a torture for the mind." One day, however, back in Hamburg, Axel notices that the compass needle points south instead of north, and he realizes that the electrical storm in the earth's interior must have reversed the instrument's poles. The final mystery is explained, the puzzle is complete, and, in a version of the lived-happily-ever-after formula, Axel tells us that "from that day onward, my uncle was the happiest of scientists" (p. 254).

This coda affirms the materialistic faith that the book of nature is readable to the last word, that nature is merely a cryptogram to be decoded or, as Axel puts it, that "however great the wonders of Nature may be, they can always be explained by physical laws." And yet, despite this explicit positivistic affirmation, the narrative's romance structure suggests a more problematic view. Here "explaining nature" is represented by the idea of reaching the center, which of course the explorers never do attain. Did Arne Saknussemm ever in fact reach the center? Throughout the story, Axel and Lidenbrock debate the question of the earth's internal temperature. Is the earth's core molten or even gaseous with a temperature of perhaps over two million degrees as Axel, the romantic, maintains? Or, as the positivistic Lidenbrock supposes, does the rise in temperature experienced as one descends into the earth reach a limit at a certain depth, leaving a core that can be explored by human beings? So far as the explorers descend the temperature remains comfortable, but the ultimate issue of whether the center itself is transcendently hot is never resolved, and in the narrative this debate becomes equivalent to the question of how nature can be known. Is the center literally reachable, as Lidenbrock passionately believes? Or, as Axel's dream implies, is it in fact a magical place attainable only in dream or in vision or in fiction?

Journey to the Centre of the Earth can be taken as representative of all those narratives in which the nonhuman is projected as existing "out there." Sometimes the nonhuman is an inanimate object such as Wells's intruding planet or a physical locale — the interior of the earth, the surface of the moon, the farthest reaches of the galaxy — and sometimes it is animate, an "alien" such as Wells's Martians. There is a logical continuity between stories of natural exploration and stories of alien contact. Frequently explorers will encounter animated embodiments of the alien landscape such as, say, the deadly sunflowers in Larry Niven's *Ringworld* (1970). Sometimes, too, an inanimate landscape will come alive, as in Arthur C. Clarke's *Rendezvous with Rama* (1973) where a mysteriously empty spaceship that the human protagonists are investigating suddenly begins to produce "biological robots." But even when the nonhuman remains more or less strictly inanimate, the romance form, which requires an antagonist, will nearly always result in some degree of metaphorical animation, as when the earth vomits Verne's explorers from its body. Understanding how narratives of natural exploration pass by degrees into narratives of alien contact helps to define the logical position of such stories as Olaf Stapledon's *Star Maker* (1937), Fred Hoyle's *The Black Cloud* (1957), or Gregory Benford's and Gordon Eklund's *If the Stars Are Gods* (1977) in which nebulae, stars, and other features of the cosmic landscape turn out to be alive and sentient. The possibility of a class of stories such as these, a class that might be said to be located exactly midway between fictions of inanimate nature such as *Journey to the Centre of the Earth* and alien-contact fictions such as *The War of the Worlds*, is implicit in the structure of the genre.

The narrative activity in fictions conceived primarily in the spatial category will generally be one of two kinds. Sometimes, as in *Journey to the Centre of the Earth,* man penetrates the nonhuman sphere, but equally often, as in "The Star," it is the nonhuman that is the active force, thrusting itself disruptively into the human sphere. Whether humanity is presented as active or as passive is obviously important in shaping the fiction's view of man's position in the world — Verne characteristically conceives man as heroic and active, Wells as vulnerable and passive — but, whatever the conceptual content, the general area of fictional concern remains the same. Moreover, underlying nearly all science fiction in which the nonhuman is projected spatially, we normally find some version of the Pascalian vertigo, either the terror of the void or exaltation in the contemplation of the freedom of infinite space.

The War of the Worlds, which is the best known and most influential of all alien-contact stories, is a Darwinian fable, depicting an interplanetary struggle for survival. Wells chooses as his narrator a philosophical writer who is at work on a series of papers prophesying the development of moral ideas as civilization progresses. The Martian invasion interrupts the narrator's work in midsentence, evidently just as he was about to sketch an advanced and humane future; instead of a version of utopia, the narrator is compelled to portray the collapse of society and the reduction of men to anonymous creatures, scrabbling like animals to remain alive. Wells's theme here, as in *The Time Machine* and many of his early stories, is the terrible fragility of civilization, of all that we consider humane, when seen in the larger context of such brutal natural forces as the evolutionary process.

The Pascalian terror of the void, however, is no less important in *The War of the Worlds* than the idea of evolution. Observing Mars through a telescope, Wells's narrator describes the planet as a tiny warm light:

It seemed such a little thing, so bright and small and still, faintly marked with transverse stripes, and slightly flattened from the perfect round. But so little it was, so silvery warm — a pin's head of light! It was as if it quivered, but really this was the telescope vibrating with the activity of the clockwork that kept the planet in view.[9]

The narrator goes on to remind us of "the immensity of vacancy in which the dust of the material universe swims" and to invoke the "unfathomable darkness" of space: "You know how that blackness looks on a frosty starlight night. In a telescope it seems far profounder" (p. 312). The contrast drawn here between light and darkness, warmth and cold, quivering movement and vacancy, is ultimately a contrast between life and death: the "unfathomable darkness" of space is also the mystery of nonbeing, and the passage as a whole suggests the preciousness and the fragility of life in a universe that is mostly empty.

Life and death are the terms in conflict in *The War of the Worlds*. Despite its vital appearance in the telescope, Mars is a dying planet. Older than the earth, its oceans are evaporating, its atmosphere is dissipating, and the entire planet is cooling, moving toward the chill of death. Observing the earth, the Martians see a planet teeming with life, a "warmer planet, green with vegetation and grey with water, with a cloudy atmosphere eloquent of fertility" (p. 310). To preserve themselves they undertake to invade the earth.

From one point of view, Mars and the Martians are a precious speck of life in the universe. From another, however, they are the agents of death. The novel opens with a description of the Martians studying mankind from across the gulf of space even as a man with a microscope might study the minuscule creatures in a drop of water. "With infinite complacency men went to and fro over this globe about their little affairs," while millions of miles away on Mars, "minds that are to our minds as ours are to those of the beasts that perish, intellects vast and cool and unsympathetic, regarded this earth with envious eyes, and slowly and surely drew their plans against us" (p. 309). The contrast between the greatness of the Martian intelligence and the littleness of mankind that dominates the novel's opening recalls the familiar contrast between the greatness of the cosmos and human littleness. Indeed, what Wells has done is to transfer the usual attributes of the physical cosmos – vastness, coldness, indifference – to the Martians. Significantly, the Martians in their fighting machines dwarf men physically, even as their great brains dwarf ours intellectually. Their weapons – the heat ray, the poison gas – are depersonalizing instruments of mass slaughter, and attempts to communicate with them are as fruitless as if they were literally a force of nature. The Martians have consciousness and will, but they are not unlike the intruding planetoid in "The Star" in their absolute unconcern for mankind.

Wells's Martians thus fuse the Darwinian and the Pascalian themes, and the conception of the black void of space informs the whole narrative. Much of the fable's power, however, derives from the richness with which Wells develops the Martians as fairy-tale figures of death. Physically feeble as a result of their extreme evolution and the unaccustomed gravity of earth, the Martians move painfully and slowly like dying creatures. Only their eyes, the signs of their intelligence, are intense and vital. Their strength comes from their elaborate machines, mechanisms that are, like themselves, grotesque images of life in death. At one point the narrator describes these machines in detail, emphasizing the way they seem more alive than their masters:

It is remarkable that the long leverages of their machines are in most cases actuated by a sort of sham musculature of disks in an elastic sheath; these disks become polarised and drawn closely and powerfully together when traversed by a current of electricity. In this way the curious parallelism to animal motions, which was so striking and disturbing to the human beholder, was attained. Such quasi-muscles abounded in the crablike handling-machine which, on my first peeping out of the slit, I watched unpacking the cylinder. It seemed infinitely more alive than the actual Martians lying beyond it in the sunset light, panting, stirring ineffectual tentacles, and moving feebly after their vast journey across space.   (p. 412).

But the Martians are also vampires, maintaining their feeble existence by draining other creatures' blood. Moreover, the color red with which they are repeatedly associated – Mars is of course the red planet, the Martian vegetation that takes hold on the earth is red, and the heat ray turns everything it touches lurid red with flame – hints of the diabolic. Metaphorically, the Martians are fiends, and such passages as the description of the alien outpost lit by the "vivid red glare" of flames against which the Martians appear in silhouette as "huge black shapes, grotesque and strange" suggest the way they transform the English countryside into the landscape of hell.

The diabolic red – often the color is "blood red" – is related to the evolutionary theme, suggesting the bloody competition in which one species is another's food. Through the heat ray and its fires, the color is also associated with the pattern of references to temperature – the earth is neither hot nor cold but benevolently warm – and thus with the cosmic theme, reminding us of the narrow range of conditions in which life is possible. In the novel's striking color pattern, red is opposed both to black, the color of the void and of death, and to green and gray or blue, the colors of the living earth and by extension of life generally. Appropriately, given the characterization of the Martian machines as a form of sham life, the falling cylinders appear in the sky as greenish streaks, and the digging and refining machines produce flickering green fire and puffs of green smoke.

The narrative of the Martian invasion, the story of the apparently inevitable triumph of death over life, reaches a climax in the chapter titled "Dead London" in which the narrator, having survived his imprisonment in the ruined house and met and parted from the artilleryman, arrives in a desolate urban landscape of black dust and corpses, a "city of the dead" lying in "its black shroud" (p. 441). In South Kensington he hears the sound of a Martian howling, "Ulla, ulla, ulla, ulla," and soon discovers that the invaders have succumbed to earthly bacteria, antagonists for which they were wholly unprepared. The Martians' sudden overthrow is anticipated by a number of earlier references to bacteria, but above all we are reminded of the novel's opening and the image there of the Martians studying us from a distance "as a man with a microscope might scrutinise the transient creatures that swarm and multiply in a drop of water." The teeming microbes, flashing through their minimal existences, signify the ultimate units of life; in effect they stand for the vital principle itself.[10] By employing them to defeat the Martians the text not only emphasizes human insignificance but also reaffirms that all along it has been concerned with an opposition broader and more encompassing than the particular struggle between the Martians and ourselves. Related to this reaffirmation of the broader concerns is the shift in the perception of the invaders that occurs when the narrator hears the "sobbing alternation" of the dying Martian's cry. "It was," he says, "as if that mighty desert of houses had found a voice for its fear and solitude" (p. 441). When the cry ceases the narrator states directly that the wailing represented a kind of companionship: "By virtue of it London had still seemed alive, and the sense of life about me had upheld me." What Wells has done, as a recent commentator shrewdly notes, is to transpose the developing tragedy of the human race into a tragedy of the Martians.[11] The transposition is both aesthetically satisfying — closure is achieved through the surprising fulfillment of our expectations of tragedy — and significant. Once again, as at the opening, the Martians are aligned with life rather than death, are seen as precious fragments of sentience in a universe of hostile vacancy.

The ending thus hints at a kind of tragic fraternity between men and Martians. Nevertheless, the text suggests that we must be cautious about how completely we share the narrator's moment of identification with the aliens. The narrator hears the final howl as a kind of sobbing, and he speaks of the Martian dying "even as it had been crying to its companions." But earlier we have been told that the Martians are probably telepathic and that their sounds are in no way connected with communication. Moreover, the repeated characterization of the Martians as emotionless figures of cold intellect should make us realize that here the narrator is projecting his own feelings onto the aliens, attributing human characteristics to creatures fundamentally different from ourselves. After the death of the Martians, the narrator also lapses into what is for him an unusual rush of religious emotion, invoking God's wisdom and the story of Jehovah's decimation of King Sennacherib's army in order to protect the chosen people, and finally extending his hands to the sky in gratitude to the Lord. Oddly, at this moment the narrator sounds almost like the provincial curate whose inability to transcend his inappropriate religious conceptions results in madness. All through the novel Wells has been concerned with the difficulty of achieving and sustaining an adequate conception of the Martians and of the threat they pose. The curate is the most obvious example of Wells's concern with this issue, but the artilleryman too, as the novel gradually reveals, is as much driven by self-aggrandizing fantasies and by petty class resentments — "There won't be any more Royal Academy of Arts, and no nice little feeds at restaurants" — as by a genuine grasp of the situation, and, despite his fine talk, he finally lapses into self-indulgence and inaction. We are all, the novel suggests, limited in our understanding of things by the pettiness of our lives, and we all find it difficult to come to grips with a truly indifferent universe, one neither arranged on a human model nor constructed on a human scale.

The Martians are by far the most interesting figures

in Wells's novel, and the conception of them is central
to the fiction in a way that the particular conception
of the narrator or the artilleryman is not. At one level
the Martians are signs that stand for the idea of alienness, the idea of the incomprehensible otherness of the
universe in which man lives. At another level, however,
they stand for ourselves. In the evolutionary fable, for
example, the Martians with their hypertrophied brains
and atrophied bodies suggest a possible human future.
Alluding to Wells's own popular essay on future evolution, "The Man of the Year Million," the narrator mentions that, long before the Martian invasion, a quasi-
scientific writer suggested that man might evolve into
just such creatures as the Martians. The narrator goes
on to remark that "without the body the brain would,
of course, become a mere selfish intelligence, without
any of the emotional substratum of the human being"
(p. 410), and thus he makes explicit another dimension
of metaphorical significance, this time a specifically
moral one in which the Martians represent the eternal
danger of cold reason divorced from humane feeling.

The Martians also have political significance, and
once again the narrator makes this dimension explicit,
comparing the Martian colonization of the earth to the
European extermination of the Tasmanians. We can
perhaps read an even more fundamental, though less
explicit, political meaning in the fiction if we consider
the Martians as a metaphorical projection of the capi-
talistic industrial system of the late nineteenth century,
here conceived as a social machine created by a
ruthless economic reason that sucks the lifeblood out
of human beings. Such a reading would emphasize the

Martians' inaccessibility, their failure to respond to human attempts at communication, and their reduction of mankind to degraded and anonymous masses. It would find new and ironic meaning in the image of the machines as seemingly more alive than the actual Martians. And it would emphasize, too, the artilleryman's description of the petty clerks, fearful of being dismissed from jobs in businesses they did not understand, fearful of their wives and of criminals in the back streets, concerned principally with securing a little bit of money to make for safety in "their one little miserable skeddadle through the world." Such already dead souls, the artilleryman suggests, would be delighted to be the Martians' cattle: after a while they would even wonder how people survived before there were Martians to take care of them.

Wells's Martians raise fundamental questions about the portrayal of aliens — and, indeed, of the nonhuman generally — in literature. Is it possible to avoid projecting human characteristics onto the alien? Is it possible, in other words, to portray a truly alien creature, one wholly different from ourselves?

If alien creatures are ever encountered, the problem of how to comprehend them will be a matter for science. Fiction, however, is not an instrument of inquiry of the same order as physics or biology. The question here is not one of knowledge — can we know the nonhuman? — but one of representation. As Patrick Parrinder suggests, it is not possible to imagine something utterly alien but only to conceive of something as alien by contrast or analogy with something already known. Thus we may imagine flying pigs or ambulatory brains or even intelligent stars, but we cannot imagine something that bears no relationship at all to what we already know. Since the literary alien must always be constructed on some principle of analogy or contrast with our world, it follows that the truly alien can never be actualized in a text. The alien can be gestured toward — the text can provide signs that represent the idea of alienness — but the alien itself in its radical otherness cannot be directly portrayed. Moreover, the choice of alien features is always significant. Through his aliens, a science-fiction writer is inevitably, at least in part, writing about his own world, and it is precisely this that makes the aliens in science fiction so fascinating. As Parrinder indicates and as the case of Wells's Martians affirms, aliens in science fiction always possess a metaphorical dimension.[12]

Perhaps we can regard the problem faced by the science-fiction writer attempting to write about the nonhuman as analogous to that of the religious writer attempting to portray the divine. Like those medieval playwrights who bring even God the Father onstage in the person of an actor, the science-fiction writer may choose to suppress the fact that his aliens are projections of the human world. Alternatively, the writer may in some fashion acknowledge the inevitable limitation inherent in the literary form, as Milton does in *Paradise Lost* when he describes the struggle between God and Satan as an epic battle.

H. G Wells's self-conscious gesture toward his own "The Man of the Year Million" implicitly acknowledges the metaphorical nature of his Martians; indeed, it is because Wells allows the metaphorical dimensions of his aliens to develop freely that *The War of the Worlds* is so rich a fiction. Other texts acknowledge and thus in a sense free themselves from their limitations through humor. In Robert Sheckley's fine "Specialist" (1953), for instance, the aliens who land on earth constitute an organic starship that functions through a collaboration of representatives of many species, each of which has a specialized role such as Engine, Thinker, Feeder, or Eye. The starship's immediate purpose is to enlist a human being to fill the role of Pusher, the agent that accelerates the vessel to faster-than-light speeds. "Pushing," it turns out, is mankind's true vocation, the one for which we are biologically specialized, and all human unhappiness and aggression derive ultimately from our frustration at not being able to perform our proper function in the cosmic society of specialized races. Sheckley employs the point of view of the aliens, presenting them and their adventures in a broad parody of a deep-sea yarn. Thus Feeder is a youngster on his first voyage, and the Walls are described as "fine workers and good shipmates, but happy-go-lucky fellows at best."[13] This conspicuous and comic anthropomorphizing enables Sheckley to avoid the pitfalls of any solemn attempt at a direct portrayal of the alien and ensures that the text will be read as a parable rather than as a jejune description of the true nature of the universe. From Edgar Rice Burroughs to Larry Niven, however, the majority of popular science-fiction writers have pretended to present "genuine" protrayals of the alien. This is not necessarily to say that all such fictions are ineffective.

ALIEN ENCOUNTERS

Some of them — Robert Heinlein's *The Puppet Masters* (1951), for example — have an authentic, if primitive, power that derives in part precisely from the suppression of fairly obvious connections with our world. But, compared to *The War of the Worlds* or to "Specialist," such fictions generally seem naive.

In my first chapter I distinguished between primary and secondary phases of science fiction's development. We can observe now that the characteristic treatment of the alien in secondary science fiction — that is, the body of writing that can take the existence of the science-fiction genre for granted — is not particularly self-conscious. In fact, most of these texts are less self-conscious than Wells's *The War of the Worlds*, which confirms that literary sophistication, as such, is not simply a function of the process of generic development. The "secondariness" of these texts characteristically manifests itself in their reaction against the pulp stereotype of the hostile alien, a stereotype that of course derives ultimately from Wells's Martians. Thus we get fictions such as Arthur C. Clarke's interesting *Childhood's End* (1953) in which the aliens are beneficent even though they look like devils, and a whole host of lesser fables in which salvation comes to mankind in the form of aliens from outer space. Other stories react against the primitive science-fiction monsters by portraying aliens that are neither "good" nor "bad" but conspicuously like ourselves. The best known of these is Murray Leinster's "First Contact" (1945) in which human and alien starships meeting in deep space consider the problem of how each is to return home without revealing the location of its home planet to a potential enemy. The solution is to exchange ships, with each crew making sure that its own ship has no capacity to trace the other. The story reaffirms its basic point about the aliens when it concludes with the human communications officer revealing that he spent the time while the ships were being prepared for exchange in conversation with his alien counterpart swapping dirty jokes.

The logic of generic development leads, as I suggested earlier, to interiorization and to emphatic metaphorization in which spiritual or psychological correlatives replace simple external action. Ursula K. Le Guin's justly celebrated *The Left Hand of Darkness* (1969) is such a "late" treatment of the alien-contact theme. Here the theme becomes quite explicitly a metaphor for any contact between people of different cultures or of different sexes or, indeed, for any kind of human contact at all. In fact, Le Guin's aliens, the Gethenians, are not true aliens at all, but only an exotic branch of the human race. However, even as the alien-contact theme in the foreground is humanized and made figurative, the nonhuman reappears in the background, deanimated and displaced onto the setting, the inhospitably frigid planet Gethen or Winter, which represents a version of the same cold and uncaring universe that Wells animated in the form of his Martians. What Le Guin has done, in effect, is to shift the focus of the story that Wells presents in both "The Star" and *The War of the Worlds* from the nonhuman to the human. But the general area of concern remains the same and, in Le Guin as in Wells, the importance of human brotherhood when seen against the background of the void is self-evident.

ALIEN ENCOUNTERS

The most radical, and for my purposes the most interesting, late treatment of the alien-contact theme is Stanislaw Lem's *Solaris* (1961). Like Le Guin, Lem shifts the focus from the nonhuman to the human. He does so, however, not so much by making the whole situation of contact metaphorical as by forming his narrative precisely around the problem of anthropomorphization, the problem of coming to grips with or even conceiving something truly nonhuman. In Lem's hands, cosmology, the traditional concern of science fiction in the space category, yields to epistemology, an exploration of the limitations inherent in any human frame of reference. His strategy is to turn the science-fiction genre with its usually unexamined romantic-heroic and religious structures back upon itself. The result is a highly self-conscious fiction that is as much a work of generic criticism as it is a new text in the genre.

Most science-fiction narratives follow Wells in employing as their signs of the nonhuman figures that are clearly recognizable as versions of ourselves. Lem's initial move in *Solaris* is to choose as problematic a sign of the nonhuman as possible. Thus the mysterious ocean that dominates the novel is a figure precisely located on the border between inanimate nature and animate creature. On the one hand, the ocean is an unusual extraterrestrial landscape, a colloidal sea covering an entire planet. But, on the other, it appears able to manipulate such fundamental physical properties as gravity and to respond to stimuli in remarkable ways. Does the ocean think? Does it have desires or emotions? Is it, in other words, merely an extraordinary natural phenomenon or a living creature?

82

By making Solaris itself unyieldingly problematic,
Lem shifts the narrative emphasis from the object to
the process of inquiry. For nearly a century the ocean
has been the subject of intensive study, and an entirely
new field of investigation, Solaristics, has developed in
the attempt to answer fundamental questions about
the planet. But, although a massive library of scholarship has been generated, little if any real progress has
been made. Large sections of the novel consist of
detailed and often funny accounts of the various
theories that have been proposed about the planet. Do
the huge and fantastic forms that the ocean continually generates — Giese, an early student of Solaris, gave
these formations such names as "mimoids," "sym-
metriads," and "asymmetriads" — represent the physical
basis of unimaginably advanced and complex thought?
Or are they the anarchic death throes of a dying
creature? Has the ocean failed to respond to human
overtures because it is serenely contemptuous of mankind? Or, being a gargantuan creature, has it simply
failed to notice men at all?

As the novel proceeds, the inquiry turns more and
more emphatically into an analysis of the human
motives behind the whole Solarist enterprise and thus,
implicitly, also into an analysis of science fiction and
its analogous concern with the nonhuman. "We think
of ourselves as the Knights of the Holy Contact," says
Snow, one of the scientists stationed on the planet.
But such heroic notions are inappropriate, for mankind
actually has no interest in the nonhuman: "We are only
seeking Man. We have no need of other worlds. We
need mirrors. We don't know what to do with other

83

worlds."[14] And late in the novel we hear about the scholar Muntius, who regards the Solarist enterprise as "the space era's equivalent of religion: faith disguised as science." After all, what kind of contact could there be with anything so alien as the ocean? According to Muntius, "Solaristics is a revival of long-vanished myths, the expression of mystical nostalgias which men are unwilling to confess openly. The cornerstone is deeply entrenched in the foundations of the edifice: it is the hope of Redemption" (p.180).

Lem attempts to keep his sign of the nonhuman as empty, as nonreferential, as possible, and thus he prevents the metaphorical dimensions of his alien from developing freely in the manner of Wells. Nevertheless, because he must employ some sign, must portray the nonhuman as "this" rather than "that," not even Lem can entirely avoid metaphor. In selecting the sea as a sign, Lem employs a familiar image of the nonhuman, one already invested by ancient usage from Homer and Shakespeare to Melville and Verne with the idea of the infinite. Moreover, instead of suppressing the sea's traditional attributes of mysteriousness and vastness, Lem insists upon them repeatedly, as when we are told that, precisely because of its complexity, the pattern of a symmetriad is incomprehensible: "We observe a fraction of the process, like hearing the vibration of a single string in an orchestra of super-giants. We know, but cannot grasp, that above and below, beyond the limits of perception or imagination, thousands and millions of simultaneous transformations are at work" (pp.129-130). Like the abysses in *Journey to the Centre of the Earth* or the Martians in

The War of the Worlds, the enigmatic Solaris ocean can be understood as a version of the infinite void, a metaphor for the vast and unknown universe.

Interestingly, Lem's protagonist, Kris Kelvin, twice has dreams reminiscent of Axel's crucial daydream in which, sweeping backward into the abyss of time, he finally loses himself in infinity. Axel's dream is an ecstatic vision. Kelvin's dreams, however, are nightmares, brutal embodiments of the Pascalian terror and the basic fear of disintegration of the self:

I seemed to be growing smaller, and the invisible sky, horizonless, the formless immensity of space, without stars, receded, extended and grew bigger all around me. I tried to crawl out of bed, but there was no bed; beneath the cover of darkness there was a void. I pressed my hands to my face. I no longer had any fingers or any hands. I wanted to scream . . .   (p. 99)

The later dream, part of a series of powerful visions that Kelvin suspects may have been directly influenced by the ocean, is more complex. Presented in terms that distantly echo Genesis, it incorporates a vision first of the creation of a self out of formless substance in "the heart of vastness," then of the making of a companion for the self, and finally of a dissolution back into the void during which the consciousness remains horrifyingly intact, howling soundlessly, "begging for death and for an end" (pp. 186-188).

Understanding the Pascalian terror that informs the narrative helps to explain the various protective enclosures, similar in significance to the closed and safe spaces characteristic of Verne's fictions, that are so prominent in *Solaris*. The novel begins, for example, with Kelvin being sealed first in the pneumatic envelope of a space suit and then in a small metal capsule for the faster-than-light journey through "the pale reddish glow of infinity" to Solaris. The goal of his journey is another enclosure, the Solaris station, hovering safely, like Swift's Laputa, above the ocean's surface. And the station itself is a nest of further enclosures — cabins, laboratory, cold storage chamber — each a special and bounded territory marked by a door, often a locked door. Many of the chambers have windows through which at times the mysterious ocean can be viewed. As in Verne, the window upon the infinite defines insideness and enclosure by opposition, but here windows, lights, spectacles, and other instruments related to seeing also suggest the novel's epistemological concern: How can we truly "see" the nonhuman? Whenever the brighter of Solaris's two suns rises, the men must don dark glasses until automatic metal shutters seal the windows closed. Moreover, located in the heart of the station, the library that is the repository of accumulated Solarist scholarship is signficantly windowless. As the image of the library suggests, intellectual structures also can be a form of enclosure, and the huge monument of scholarly effort encapsulated in the station's center clearly functions as much to separate mankind from the ocean as to open a window onto its mystery.

In Verne the feeling of enclosure is enjoyable. To sit in the coziness of the Nautilus saloon and gaze out into the mystery of the ocean is a sign of the triumph

of human endeavor and a delight. In *Solaris,* however,
where there is little sense of joy, the complex of protective barriers and enclosures seems rather to be an
expression of agoraphobia, the fear of open places.
Not until the novel's end when Kelvin steps onto the
surface of the old mimoid do any of the men venture
out of the station. Usually, in fact, they do not even
venture out of their chambers, each remaining imprisoned in a private psychological drama. Enclosures
may protect man from the infinite, but they also effectively sequester him in the limited world of the human
or, in the case of more personal enclosures, in the still
more limited world of the self. As the narrative continues, the intellectual, psychological, and physical
enclosures in which the men live come to seem more
and more oppressive, and the feeling conveyed by
the novel as a whole becomes emphatically claustro-
phobic.

 Solaris has two distinct components, the material
concerned with Solaristics, the long history of attempts
to understand and contact the ocean, and the more
particular story of Kelvin's relations with Rheya, his
dead wife. The material concerned with Solaristics is
broad in sweep and cooly intellectual in style. This
aspect of the novel might be characterized as a
philosophical fantasia on the central science-fiction
theme. The story of Kelvin and Rheya — or, rather, of
the simulacrum of Rheya, a "visitor" that the ocean
generates from Kelvin's memories — is intense and emotional. Logically, the broader story of the attempt to
make contact with the ocean constitutes the novel's
main plot and the story of Kelvin and Rheya con-

ALIEN ENCOUNTERS

stitutes the subplot, but Lem makes the broader story the background for the story of the visitors. The Solaristics material is rooted in satire: it recalls, for example, certain parts of *A Tale of a Tub* or the description of the academicians in the third book of *Gulliver's Travels*. The novel's foreground, however, is a science-fiction version of a ghost story, and it is the source of most of the book's narrative power.

The Rheya plot is tied to the broader story of Solaris by having the ocean produce her and the other visitors in response to the latest attempt to achieve contact, this time by bombarding the sea with x-rays. (What the ocean's purposes might be in sending the visitors naturally remains a mystery.) More important, the story of Rheya is a systematic development from the novel's broader concern with the human in relation to the nonhuman, for the crucial point about Rheya and the other visitors is that they are neither human nor nonhuman. In appearance the visitors seem human, and, indeed, down to the level of the molecule their bodies are indistinguishable from human bodies. Nevertheless, they are composed of a fundamentally different kind of matter from ourselves, conglomerations of neutrinos rather than atoms. They require neither food nor sleep, their tissues almost instantaneously regenerate if they are injured, and in some circumstances they possess astonishing physical strength. Most disturbing, however, they are neither monsters nor puppets, but fully conscious creatures capable of free will who have at first no idea that they are anything but the human beings they resemble. What Lem has done in introducing the visitors is to allow the human versus nonhuman opposition to generate a third term on the boundary between the two categories. And by introducing this third term he has rendered problematic the fundamental opposition that enables his fiction — and the science-fiction genre in general — to exist.

Faced with the utterly alien ocean, human categories of thought break down. Giese, the first great student of Solaris, was a scholarly classifier. But, although he tried to remain scrupulously objective in his descriptions, Giese's taxonomy of Solarian forms was, as Kelvin remarks, inevitably shot through with geocentric thinking, with inappropriate extensions of the familiar world. Likewise, faced with the visitors, the men stationed on Solaris must confront an impossible problem in definition and classification, one hopelessly complicated by the fact that the visitors are erotic figures drawn from the deepest realms of the scientists' emotional beings. In Kelvin's case, Rheya, who committed suicide when Kelvin abandoned her, is a figure of intense guilt as well as love. Dealing with the visitors is thus always an emotional matter, and, since the visitors are conscious beings who regard themselves as human, the question of how to deal with them is also a problem with a moral dimension.

When Kelvin arrives on Solaris the visitors have already been appearing for some time. One of the men on the station, Gibarian, has committed suicide, and the other two, Snow and Sartorius, have retreated in various ways into isolation. Suggestively, Gibarian's body has been stored in a freezer. As we have seen both in *Journey to the Centre of the Earth* and in *The*

ALIEN ENCOUNTERS

War of the Worlds temperature is often significant in
science fiction. Patterns of heat and cold generally
refer in some way to the modern, alienated sense of
the narrow range of physical conditions in which
human life is possible and thus to the cosmic theme of
the indifferent universe. In *Solaris,* however, the
temperature motif has become metaphorical. Kelvin,
whose name evokes the Kelvin scale for measuring
temperature, repeatedly complains that the station is
stifling, but evidently the problem is not simply
physical, for here the feeling of oppressive heat and
the associated appearances of Solaris' glowing red sun
correspond to increases in the temperature of the
novel's emotional climate. Nevertheless, life and death
are still very much the issue, and the body in the
freezer implies that Gibarian chose the cold of death
rather than continuing to try to bear the heat of a
situation beyond the range of human endurance. Snow
is also in a sense dead, having lapsed into cynicism
and slovenly inactivity. Sartorius, on the other hand,
like the man who dresses for dinner in the heat of the
jungle, responds to extreme situations by clinging rigidly to normality, attempting to eliminate anything
that intrudes upon his orderly world. Formal and
pedantic, he refuses to acknowledge any personal or
emotional involvement with the visitors – indeed, he
refuses to acknowledge the whole personal side of
life – and he is energetically at work upon a device to
destroy them.

Gibarian, Snow, and Sartorius represent an
anatomy of manifestly inadequate responses to the
visitors. What would an adequate response be? When

Rheya appears, Kelvin initially reacts somewhat in the manner of Sartorius, insistently reminding himself that this is not the real Rheya and finally trapping the visitor aboard a space capsule and launching it into orbit. If eliminated, new versions of the visitors return as if nothing had happened, and when a duplicate Rheya appears, Kelvin, now behaving somewhat like Snow, cynically welcomes her as his wife. But what begins as a charade becomes reality as Kelvin falls in love with Rheya all over again, accepting her as if she were indeed a human being and his wife. Eventually Rheya discovers what she is. Horrified by the knowledge but even more appalled at the pain her presence is causing Kelvin, she attempts to commit suicide. Lem has thus driven the story into an excruciating moral and philosophical paradox. Rheya is not human; she is an emanation of the ocean and her presence is indeed torture to Kelvin. Nevertheless, she truly loves him and means to kill herself for his sake. Can such love be anything but human?

Kelvin allowed the real Rheya to kill herself; this time he does everything he can to keep Rheya from self-destruction. But is his heroic love appropriate? Is he not, as Snow in an important conversation maintains, naive in believing that he will be a traitor if he lets Rheya destroy herself and a good man if he keeps her? Is he not projecting moral categories into a context in which human morality does not apply, falling prey to the same kind of error that has impeded Giese and the other Solarists in their study of the ocean? "What if it is not possible, here, to be anything but a traitor?" Snow asks. Kelvin protests that he loves

Rheya, this Rheya who has proved her love by trying
to kill herself. "She is willing to give her life," Snow
replies coldly. "So are you. It's touching, it's magnificent, anything you like, but it's out of place here – it's
the wrong setting" (pp. 161-162). Snow, the cool cynic,
is an unsympathetic figure compared to Kelvin, the
romantic lover. Yet we should realize that Lem has
employed the sentimental codes of the literary love
story and thus encourages us to sympathize with
Kelvin's passion only to lead us into a trap that illustrates how difficult it is to avoid inappropriate patterns of thought. Snow is correct. In embracing Rheya
as completely human, Kelvin has adopted a position
no more adequate than that of Sartorius, who merely
wishes to obliterate the visitors.

Eventually Rheya does destroy herself. Kelvin is
grief-stricken, but out of his grief emerges a new
understanding of the fallacy of his former romanticism. Like mankind in general in its romantic and
heroic attitude toward the cosmos – appropriately, the
spaceships in *Solaris* bear such names as "Prometheus"
or "Ulysses" – so Kelvin has regarded himself as a
figure in a heroic story. With unreflective Quixotism,
mankind has characteristically pursued such visionary
goals as that of the conquest of nature through the
triumphant expansion of the human race throughout
space or, in the case of Solaris, of achieving some
form of ultimate "contact" with the ocean. Moreover,
these goals have carried the force of the absolute, of
divine commands, requiring if necessary total immola-
tion in their pursuit. Kelvin, too, has been a Knight of
the Holy Contact and, partially in expiation of his

former lack of chivalry toward her, Rheya's own true champion and protector. But now, meditating upon his future without Rheya, Kelvin realizes that, although he will develop new interests and occupations, he will not give himself completely to them. Indeed, he discovers that he will never again give himself completely to anything or anybody. "And this future Kelvin," he insists, "will be no less worthy a man than the Kelvin of the past, who was prepared for anything in the name of an ambitious enterprise called Contact" (p. 203).

Having renounced romantic absolutes in his own life, Kelvin attempts to extend the implications of his new understanding into the realm of cosmology or, more accurately, into theology. A universe in which absolute goals make sense must contain a god to authenticate those goals, and mankind has indeed behaved as if such an absolute god exists. But what kind of universe can ratify his new understanding of the contingency of all commitments? As an answer, Kelvin develops and explains to Snow his hypothesis of an imperfect god, a limited and evolving god who develops in the course of time. "Man does not create gods, in spite of appearances," Kelvin says: "The times, the age, impose them on him" — by which he means that the idea of a particular kind of god is not derived from an uncircumscribed act of wish fullfillment, but is the product of an age's understanding of things. Given his disillusionment, his renunciation of romantic absolutes, the only kind of god that Kelvin can even imagine believing in is one that is limited in omniscience and power, "a god whose passion is not a redemption, who saves nothing, fulfills no purpose — a god who simply is" (pp. 205-206).

Kelvin's theological conversation with Snow is to be read less as direct religious speculation than as an indirect restatement of his new freedom from heroic illusions. The conversation ends abruptly with the sighting of a very old mimoid and Kelvin's decision to venture outside the station and explore it. "When I get back to Earth," he explains, "I don't want to have to confess that I'm a Solarist who has never set foot on Solaris!" Kelvin's act of going outside is of course suggestive, as is the image of the old and already fragmenting mimoid which perhaps reflects the disintegrating model of reality that has dominated both mankind's heroic age of conquest and Kelvin's romantic youth. Once outside, Kelvin realizes that he is not really interested in the mimoid; his purpose is to acquaint himself with the ocean. Walking to the edge of the sea, he extends his gloved hand toward a wave and experiences a phenomenon noted a century earlier: "the wave hesitated, recoiled, enveloped my hand without touching it, so that a thin covering of 'air' separated my glove inside a cavity which had been fluid a moment previously, and now had a fleshly consistency." When he raises his hand the enveloping substance rises with it, forming a kind of flower. Stretched beyond a certain limit, however, the flower trembles and falls back into the main body of the waiting wave. Kelvin repeats the game several times until the ocean, "as if bored with a too familiar sensation," ceases to respond. Then he sits down, disturbed by the phenomenon, but feeling "somehow changed" by the "experience as I had lived it" (pp. 209-210).

The game Kelvin plays with the ocean recapitulates

the transforming experience that he has had in the novel. Delicately, the flowerlike extension that molds itself to Kelvin's hand recalls Rheya, who also retreated back into the wave when stretched beyond her limit. The game is thus a retrospective image and, as such, contributes to the achievement of narrative closure. But it also serves as a confirmation that the nonhuman really exists, that beyond ourselves is something that is not ourselves, and as a reminder of the problematic nature of any interaction with the genuinely alien. Sitting on the "beach," sign of the boundary between the two modes of existence, the human and the nonhuman, Kelvin decides not to return to earth after all but to remain on Solaris. The renunciation of heroics, Lem is suggesting, need not mean the loss of purpose. Kelvin has no idea what kind of interactions with the ocean may occur in the future and no hope for Rheya's return. Nevertheless, he knows that the ocean is real and he is willing to commit himself to whatever the future may bring. "I knew nothing," he says in his final words, "and I persisted in the faith that the time of cruel miracles was not past."

TIME

Science fiction depends upon a sense of the reality of life in time, upon a sense of change and transformation and the conviction that tomorrow will be different from today. Speaking generally and oversimplifying for the sake of brevity, it would not be entirely inaccurate to say that for most of history Western thought has been dominated by one version or another of the Platonic identification of the real with the eternal and unchanging. The medieval Christian, for example, lived in a world of permanent spiritual realities. For him history was not an open-ended process leading into the unknown but a ritualized enactment of a drama in which the cosmos moved toward perfection. Moreover, for him the total extent of time, the six-thousand-year scheme of universal history abstracted from the Bible early in the Christian era, was still fundamentally human in scale. In such circumstances science fiction, dependent upon the radical sense of alienation from the cosmos, could not appear.

Like our modern sense of space, our sense of time has its roots in the Renaissance. In that period the shift in focus from the long and continuing life of the community to the evanescent moment of the individual resulted in a new sense of time as the antagonist of man, the brutal agent that devours beauty and life. Nevertheless, the fierce private wars with time such as those memorialized in Shakespeare's sonnets still took place within the embracing frame of sacramental time, time guaranteed by God the Creator and Redeemer. The first hints of the possibility of unbounded time, time inhumanly vast in scale, emerged in the seven-

96

teenth century as the logical extension of the new idea
of unbounded space. For example, in Bernard de Fon-
tenelle's *Conversations on the Plurality of Worlds*
(1686), a brilliant popularization of the Copernican
system, we learn that even stars grow old and die: it
only requires time.[1] At this moment, however, there
was no empirical evidence available to compel the
development of such hints into a new conception of
time comparable to the new idea of space. Until the
end of the eighteenth century, the biblical time
scheme was generally taken for granted. Moreover, the
normal mode of scientific and of humanistic thought,
deeply influenced by Descartes and Newton, was
markedly static and atemporal, with the emphasis
upon the fixed and eternal laws which the study both
of nature and of man revealed.

The explosion of the hoary biblical scheme of
world history came in the first third of the nineteenth
century through the discoveries of the new science of
geology, culminating in Charles Lyell's monumental
Principles of Geology (1831-1833). "He who can read Sir
Charles Lyell's grand work," wrote Darwin in the *Origin
of Species,* "and yet does not admit how vast have
been the past periods of time, may at once close this
volume."[2] And Lyell himself compared the vast extent
of time revealed by geology to the seventeenth-century
discovery of the vastness of space.[3] John Ruskin nicely
expressed the anxiety produced by this direct
challenge to a sacramental sense of time: "If only the
Geologists would let me alone, I could do very well,
but those dreadful Hammers. I hear the clink of them
at the end of every cadence of the Bible verses."[4]

ALIEN ENCOUNTERS

Within thirty years of the *Principles of Geology* the evidence of prehistoric man had begun to appear — Neanderthal man was discovered in 1856 — and, most important, Darwin had published *On the Origin of Species* (1859). Now man himself had to be viewed as a natural phenomenon developing, like the earth, through unthinkable eons of time.

The revolution in natural history associated with Lyell and Darwin was of course part of a major transformation in Western attitudes toward reality. As many writers have discussed, in the Victorian period the historical or evolutionary perspective rapidly invaded nearly every area of thought from economics to philology. Again oversimplifying for brevity, we can say that the nineteenth century redefined reality as the historical process of becoming.[5] But becoming what? In the earlier part of the century the idea of progress — technological progress, social progress, spiritual progress — served almost as a form of substitute religion: the nature of history was continual betterment. In the latter part of the century, however, a multitude of factors including the revolution in natural history contributed to the waning of any automatic conviction of progress. Paradoxically, it was the discovery that man is part of nature that led to the characteristically modern alienation from nature. The vastness of space had been understood for nearly two hundred years, but it was only in the context of the discovery of the complementary vastness of time that the feeling of radical disconnection became urgent. Over the course of evolutionary time innumerable species had disappeared into oblivion. What certainty could there be that man's fate would be any different? Any sense of purpose or meaning in the process of time was at best obscure. Nature, red in tooth and claw, shrieked at Tennyson: "I care for nothing, all shall go."

Just as science fiction can be understood as an attempt to reestablish channels of communication with the world of physical nature, so it can be understood as an attempt to restore human meaning to time. Thus we have the many fables in which the inhuman vastness of time is transformed into an antagonist with which mankind can grapple or, alternatively, those fables which, portraying the wonders of future technological or biological evolution, implicitly assert that progress is real and that time's purpose is indeed the glorification of man. Thus, too, there is the tendency of science fiction to move toward apocalpytic conclusions such as that of *The Time Machine,* visions of ultimate endings that may or may not also be visions of new beginnings. As Frank Kermode says, we create fictions of endings to give meaning to time, to transform *chronos* — mere passing time — into *kairos,* time invested with the meaning derived from its goal.[6] Time without beginning or end, undifferentiated, boundless time without meaning, is utterly inhuman time. And insofar as science fiction is committed to the humanization of time, it naturally tends toward fictions of apocalypse.

Professor Lidenbrock's journey toward the center of the earth is also a journey backward in time. Likewise, the encounter with the Martians in *The War of the*

Worlds is in a sense an encounter with our own future selves. Time in these fictions is projected spatially either as a tangible series of strata or as a measurable distance between planets. This transformation is possible because we normally conceive time as a medium analogous to space, freely substituting the one for the other, as when we say we have not seen someone in a "long time" or when we speak of one place as being "ten minutes away" from another. Our metaphors for time are spatial, just as our metaphors for space are temporal. Time and space are complementary hemispheres in a single, closed conceptual system. Thus time can be freely substituted for space in the production of science-fiction stories, becoming the medium either for a journey to alien "worlds" or the medium through which "aliens," in the form of time travelers, impinge upon our world. Indeed, nearly all science-fiction narratives that are concerned directly with time depend in some way upon the spatialization of time.

Time-travel narratives are the basic fictions in the temporal category; that is, other kinds of fictions such as the future history or the alternate history may be regarded as variants of the time-travel story. H. G. Wells's *The Time Machine* (1895) represents the simplest form of time-travel narrative, that in which time is directly substituted for space as the medium for a voyage of discovery. Moreover, as the first fiction in which travel in time was imagined to be possible through the invention of a machine, Wells's story also has a historical claim to priority. The presence of the machine, the symbol of science and rationality, points to the fable's central concern with power: through science man may be able to dominate time. But what the novel finally reveals is that any such hope is false: not man but time is the master of the universe. Indeed, in the course of the story the very title develops an ironic second meaning as we come to see mankind imprisoned in the relentless turning of history, trapped in a diabolic mechanism whose workings lead to death.

Though it, too, is indirectly concerned with time and evolution, *The War of the Worlds* is fundamentally spatial in conception. In that novel the narrative thrust is generated from the image of the Martian sphere of domination expanding through southeastern England. Thus place names — Horsell, Chobham, Woking, Richmond, Putney Hill — figure prominently, and when there is a shift in the narrative center from the primary narrator to his brother in London, it is a spatial shift. *The Time Machine,* on the other hand, is temporal in form as well as in subject. Strange though the worlds of the future are, everything that the novel describes takes place in the immediate vicinity of the traveler's laboratory. The total spatial movement of the machine, which occurs when the Morlocks capture it, is merely a few feet. Moreover, the shift in narrative center here is, appropriately, a temporal shift from the present of the nominal narrator to the past of the time traveler's story. In *The War of the Worlds* the essence of the situation, the contrast between man's smallness and the universe's vastness, is evident from the beginning, and the novel consists primarily of an expansion of this initial idea. In *The Time Machine* the narrative enacts a gradual process of discovery in which mystery after mystery must be comprehended.[7]

ALIEN ENCOUNTERS

The Pascalian vertigo has a temporal counterpart. We recall, for instance, Axel's vision of falling into the abyss of past time. The "helpless headlong motion" of Wells's time traveler plunging into the future is strikingly similar. Repeatedly, the traveler speaks of "the sickness and confusion that comes with time travelling," emphasizing the machine's "sickly jarring and swaying," and, above all, "the feeling of prolonged falling."[8] In fact, the idea of the journey as an extended and sickening fall may be taken as the novel's primal image. It manifests itself in the notion of future evolution as a long fall back into the darkness of the sea and in a host of particular details such as the sloping cases and floors of the museum or the image of the planets falling back into the sun. The traveler's plummet forward in time is thus the structural equivalent of the spreading Martian sphere.

In the Eloi-Morlock section, the forward movement of the temporal plunge is displaced into the cognitive realm. Here, instead of literal movement in time, we have the traveler's intellectual movement through a series of hypotheses about the world of 802701 A.D. First, knowing only the Eloi, he guesses that the complete conquest of nature has led to the present decadence. Next he discovers the Morlocks and develops a new theory: in time the distinction between the leisured and the working classes has led to separate species with the Morlocks' labor sustaining the Eloi. Finally, after his descent to the underworld, he discovers that the Morlocks are the dominant species. Thus the plunge continues in the descent to the bottom of the Morlock shafts: the discovery of truth involves penetrating depths.

At one level the Eloi-Morlock section is a Swiftian satire on the perversity of class distinctions. Reading the novel from this point of view we might wish to discuss the irony implicit in the way that the traveler completely identifies with the Eloi, remaining blind to the bonds – meat eating, love of machinery – that tie him also to the Morlocks. But more than social satire is involved in the Eloi-Morlock section, and, from another point of view, the traveler's revulsion from the Morlocks is approriate. As in *The War of the Worlds,* the ultimate terms in conflict in *The Time Machine* are life and death. Just as the ghoulish Martians may be understood as the agents of death, embodiments of the cosmic void, so the Morlocks, whose name hints at *mors* or death as well as imprisonment, may be read as figures of living death, embodiments of the ghoulish power of devouring time. Both the Martians and the Morlocks are associated with machines and with the eating of people. Furthermore, like the coldly intellectual Martians, the Morlocks, whose qualities are in part established by their opposition to the affectionate Eloi, are devoid of sympathy. Whitish in color – white and black are the colors of death in *The Time Machine* – the traveler at one point mistakes them for ghosts. And, of course, their dark underground realm is a version of the land of the dead.

Opposed to the Morlock underworld is the neoclassical paradise of the Eloi, the land of fruits, flowers, light, and life. Here Wells draws upon the traditional idea of pastoral as a world outside of time, an evergreen land of eternal spring and youth. Significantly the Eloi, whose name is a Greek plural of the

Hebrew word for god, all appear to be children.
Pastoral paradises in literature frequently turn out to
be no less subject to time than the rest of the world.
Looming over the pretty world of the Eloi is the colos-
sal statue of the white sphinx that the traveler
discovers just beyond the bounds of the little garden in
which he lands. Winged like time and greatly eroded in
a way that "imparted an unpleasant suggestion of
disease" (p. 18), the enigmatically smiling sphinx is an
image of mortality that prefigures the traveler's
discovery of the Morlocks. *Et in Arcadia ego:* even in
Arcadia death is present.[9]

The traveler's discovery of the true relationship between the Morlocks and the Eloi foreshadows his final
discovery of time's dominance over man. But, although
the Morlocks are embodiments of time, they are also
creatures subject to time. The Eloi-Morlock section
climaxes in the forest fire and the episode on the
hillock in which the traveler finds himself surrounded
by Morlocks. At first he strikes at them with his iron
bar, but then, realizing their "absolute helplessness and
misery," he lets them be. The image of the blind,
stumbling creatures trapped on the little hill, which the
traveler calls "the most weird and horrible thing, I
think, of all that I beheld in that future age" (pp.
62-63), is a vision of the condition of all living beings
trapped in the nightmare of mortality. It summarizes
the felt meaning of the pain and incomprehension of
being in time. Unintentionally, the traveler himself with
his matches has caused the fire. The source of the
blaze is a nineteenth-century artifact just as the source
of the present state of things is to be found in nine-

teenth-century society. Blindly we contribute to the
chain of cause and effect that operates through time,
and blindly we suffer.

Recovering his machine from the white sphinx, the
traveler journeys further into the future where he
witnesses the decline of mankind's descendents into
the monstrous crabs that creep along the margin of the
sea.[10] Now the solar system itself has begun to decay,
the planets spiraling toward the cooling sun. Moreover,
the earth's revolution has become gravitationally
locked to the dying star so that the sun appears to
hang stationary on the horizon in perpetual sunset.
Finally, in the time of the black football-like creatures
of some thirty million years hence, sunset yields to
night in the eclipse that prefigures the inevitable death
of everything in the last running down of the cosmic
machine. Near to fainting, the traveler clambers onto
his own machine and returns to the gentle radiance of
the civilized present. The next day he sets off again —
whether to the past or to the future Wells's narrator is
uncertain — and on this occasion he does not return.
Just as humanity itself must eventually disappear, so
the traveler vanishes into the maw of time.

The Time Machine reveals time's supremacy over man.
In other time-travel fictions, however, man may be
conceived as more powerful than time. In Isaac
Asimov's The End of Eternity (1955) a kind of time
elevator has been established to run through the
millennia of history, and a huge bureaucracy of scientists inhabits "Eternity," a special region outside of
time. The bureaucracy's purpose is the improvement of

human well-being by initiating "reality changes." The entire course of history is kept under surveillance and, when undesirable features such as wars or inequitable social systems appear, technicians adjust history. Although the novel in effect abolishes historical time by establishing "Eternity,' nevertheless Eternity has its own history, and even there the men who are ironically called "eternals" grow old and die, wedded as they are to "physiotime." Eventually it becomes apparent that the bureaucracy's conservatism has eliminated cultural vitality — because of Eternity man has never colonized the stars — and Eternity is abolished.

Asimov's novel is a thinly disguised satire on welfare-statism and thus is almost a dystopia. But the book's energy derives less from social satire — and still less from its simplistic laissez-faire ideology — than from its vision of men able, like gods, to control time. In theme it is thus similar to Asimov's earlier *Foundation* series in which man also learns to control history through science, in this case without time travel. But *The End of Eternity* strikes a Faustian note that is absent from the *Foundation* series. Man can control time, but should he? Like much hard-core science fiction of the 1940s and 1950s, *The End of Eternity* expresses a fear not of openness — the Pascalian vertigo — but of closure. By the end the name "Eternity" ironically stands for closure, and the book concludes with an enthusiastic embracing of openness in the form of the stars that mankind will now reach.

The mechanisms — time bicycles as in Wells or time elevators as in Asimov — by which travelers journey through history point not only to the issue of power but also to the question of the mechanism of history: How do we get from here to there? Such narratives as *The Time Machine* and *The End of Eternity* generally imply an answer. In Wells's story history is the result of a dialectical interaction between man and nature; in Asimov's the interaction is between man and his institutions. In Wells the dominant power is nature, the force of entropy; in Asimov it is the human spirit that will repeatedly burst the prisons its own enterprise creates. Thus history in *The Time Machine* becomes a parabolic curve of rise and fall, whereas in *The End of Eternity* history is seen as an ascending line marked by repeated plateaus. In both cases meaning is attributed to time not only by absorbing the idea of time into the protagonist-antagonist structure of romance narrative but also by projecting a spatial pattern onto history. The shape of history becomes the meaning of history.

Instead of focusing on history's shape, however, time-travel narratives may become meditations on the distance between two points. Henry Kuttner's and C. L. Moore's "Vintage Season" (1946), for instance, deals with travelers from the future on a packaged tour of the most perfect seasons in history. Part of the appeal of the present moment is the weather — the loveliest May on record — and part is the disaster that concludes the season when a great meteor strikes the earth bringing fire and plague. The travelers are artists and connoisseurs who relish human spectacles. For them both the delight and the pain of the past are, like works of art, simultaneously real and not real. Built upon the analogy between temporal and aesthetic distance, "Vintage Season" becomes a parable of engagement and disengagement, a suggestive exploration of the processes that transform the immediacy of human experience into material for contemplation.

The visualization of time as a line generates the idea of time travel and it also generates the paradox of the time loop, the line bent back into a circle. Kuttner's and Moore's travelers remark that they are forbidden to intervene to ease the sufferings of the past because interference might alter their present. But what if a time traveler murdered his grandfather? Would the traveler himself cease to exist? If so, how could he have murdered his grandfather? Again and again, time-travel stories play with such paradoxes, working witty or bizarre variations on the theme. In *The End of Eternity* the man who developed the principle of time travel and made Eternity possible turns out to have been educated in Eternity and sent back to an earlier age precisely to develop time travel and make Eternity possible. Like the serpent eating its own tail, Eternity is forever bound in a loop of endless repetition, until reality is changed, Eternity abolished, and the imprisoning closure of repetition broken.

The spatialization of time can be understood as an aspect of the alienation of time. The effect of spatialization is to separate time from ourselves, to place it "out there" and make it subject to manipulation. And yet time is not truly equivalent to space – as Kant remarked, "Time yields no shape" – and it is not really possible to separate ourselves from time, for finally we must acknowledge that we are constituted by time. Exactly this is implicit in the paradox in which the time traveler murders his grandfather and thereby ceases to exist. Much of the fascination of the time loop is related to the fact that it represents the point at which the spatialization of time breaks down. In such circumstances time itself as we normally conceive it disappears. Thus most of the narratives that deal with the time-travel paradox are either apocalyptic visions of the abolition of time in the manner of *The End of Eternity* or explorations of the reciprocal relationship between ourselves and time. In Heinlein's "All You Zombies," for example, the protagonist's discovery that he is his own mother and father leads to a vision of utter isolation and separation. Not only is time canceled in Heinlein's fable, but the constituting opposition between self and other also collapses as the world dissolves into a phantasm, a universe of zombies in which only the self-created "I" remains as real. "I *know* where I came from," the protagonist says, "but *where did all you zombies come from?*"[11]

There is a further reason for the prominence of the time-travel paradox. As I suggested earlier, science fiction can be understood as mediating between spiritualistic and materialistic world views, between free will and determinism. We can note now that the paradox at the heart of the time loop is that both free will and determinism are asserted simultaneously, for here genuinely free agents are nevertheless caught in cycles of determined repetition. Through the time loop, then, science fiction can construct its characteristic activity in a particularly concise and provocative form.[12]

The various kinds of fictions concerned with time can be regarded as versions of the time-travel narrative.

ALIEN ENCOUNTERS

This is obvious in the case of, say, stories concerned with the temporal effects of relativity. In Poul Anderson's hyperbolic *Tau Zero* (1970) a party of interstellar voyagers finds itself caught in a nightmare of endless acceleration. Approaching ever closer to the speed of light, the ship becomes subject to greater and greater relativistic effects until millennia of cosmic time pass in mere seconds of ship's time and entire galaxies are traversed in minutes. Eventually the voyagers witness the ultimate collapse of the universe and the beginning of the next cosmic cycle in a new Big Bang. Thus relativistic effects transform the spaceship into an enormously powerful time machine.

The future-history narrative is also, logically, a time-travel fiction except that in this case the journey has usually been dropped in order not to distract from the focus on the future world. Early stories of the future such as Edward Bellamy's *Looking Backward* (1888) or H. G. Wells's *When the Sleeper Wakes* (1899) frequently include the journey motif in rudimentary form. Often the protagonist simply sleeps his way into the future in the manner of Rip Van Winkle. In another way, too, the future history betrays its relationship to the time-travel story. As Thomas A. Hanzo suggests, the story of the future involves a paradoxical linguistic game in which the actions of the future are absorbed into the past tense of narrative.[13] Indeed, the very term "future history" is an oxymoron, a linguistic analogue of the paradoxical time loop.

Stories of the near future tend to be extrapolations, extensions of selected factors from the present. Quite properly, much in these worlds remains familiar.

TIME

Stories of the far future, however, encounter an imaginative problem analogous to that of narratives that attempt to describe the alien, for the truly new is no less inconceivable than the truly alien. Stories of aliens get caught in the problem of anthropomorphism; stories of the future get caught in the problem of repetition. Hence the common phenomenon of primitive, classical, or medieval futures. Isaac Asimov's *Foundation* series is, for example, a repetition of the fall of the Roman Empire on a galactic scale, and even the pattern of *The Time Machine* is a running of the evolutionary film in reverse.

Rather than claiming to portray true or even possible futures, fictions can subvert this problem by acknowledging their futures as metaphors. For instance, Samuel R. Delany's *The Einstein Intersection* (1967), which portrays a future in which nonhuman creatures inhabit not only our planet but our mythologies, creates a world that becomes a metaphor for the experience of anyone constrained to define himself in the terms of a culture not wholly his own. And we recall Le Guin's introduction to *The Left Hand of Darkness*, a novel that also asks us not to read its world literally: "The future, in fiction, is a metaphor."

Alternatively, a story can, like *Solaris* in its incorporation of the problem of anthropomorphism, take repetition for its subject. Miller's *A Canticle for Leibowitz* portrays a postatomic war future and the gradual reemergence of technological culture through medieval and renaissance phases, climaxing again in atomic war. His theme is that those who forget the past are doomed to repeat it, and the novel is per-

111

vasively concerned with memory. It is dominated by images of repetition at every level of scale from the endlessly repeated blows that a young monk in the medieval phase is compelled to suffer to the larger pattern of recurrent war and disaster. "Listen, are we helpless," one of Miller's characters asks as the second holocaust approaches:

Are we doomed to do it again and again and again? Have we no choice but to play the Phoenix, in an unending sequence of rise and fall? Assyria, Babylon, Egypt, Greece, Carthage, Rome, the Empires of Charlemagne and the Turk. Ground to dust and plowed with salt. Spain, France, Britain, America – burned into the oblivion of the centuries. And again and again and again.[14]

The novel ends with the destruction of civilization, but also with the escape of a starship carrying a group of monks to the human colonies in space. Will mankind in space remember history and free itself from the dreadful cycles of repetition? Or are we merely witnessing the start of another and perhaps even more dreadful cycle? The novel provides no answers, and thus the meaning of the apocalyptic conclusion, and consequently of history itself, remains obscure. But, although it is tactfully silent about the nature of time's meaning – is history diabolical or divine? – the novel nevertheless asserts that, even if we cannot construe it, history is a text and time does have meaning.

Perhaps the richest of all future histories is W. Olaf Stapledon's *Last and First Men* (1930), which treats the next two billion years of history in an evolutionary

112

chronicle of the rise and fall of eighteen different species of man. Because it possesses neither characters nor, in the usual sense, plot, Stapledon's book is difficult to discuss. Moreover, deeply influenced by German romantic philosophy, particularly Hegel and Nietzsche, it is also a peculiarly abstract and ethereal text. Nevertheless, its effect on later science fiction has been great.

Last and First Men represents time in the simple principle of seriation: number follows number as the novel describes species after species, tracing man's emigration from earth to Venus and finally to Neptune. Mankind suffers drastic setbacks — on Neptune, for instance, humanity must reascend the entire evolutionary ladder — and yet the overall movement of the history is progressive, an ascent toward ever more complex human types, broader in consciousness and able to join together in increasingly comprehensive communities. The eighteenth men, for example, are not only telepathic like the fifth before them, but able at times to merge the entire race into a single vast consciousness. History's goal is the incarnation of what Hegel called Absolute Spirit, an ultimate consciousness aware of the entire cosmos at once, and mankind, we gradually realize, is Absolute Spirit in the process of becoming. Thus time is a positive force rather than a diabolical one as in Wells and, instead of imagining the experience of time as an extended fall, the novel employs the opposite metaphor, flying. Stapledon's narrator introduces this metaphor at the beginning when explaining the magnitude of his task, the presentation of eons in a single book: "Clearly we cannot walk at leisure through such a tract, in which a million terrestrial years are but as a year is to your historians. We must fly. We must travel as you do in your aeroplanes, observing only the broad features of the continent."[15] And again and again the metaphor is reintroduced, defining the experience of time as the exhilaration of soaring ever higher and taking in ever wider tracts at a glance.

Stapledon's narrator is a man of the furthest future, a member of the eighteenth species, who has assumed control of a present-day mind in order to communicate with us. "Only by some such radical and bewildering device," Stapledon says in the preface, "could I embody the possibility that there may be more in time's nature than is revealed to us." What Stapledon is here hinting — and, indeed, what the book's title, last coming before first, also hints — is that sequence is only a partial truth. The novel asks us to experience time as a sequence, a series of numbers, but at the same time it also asks us to reinterpret time as a form of space. And this process of spatialization is made explicit in the graphic time charts that punctuate the narrative and summarize it, each chart subsuming all the previous ones as our "height" increases and our vision of time encompasses progressively wider expanses. Late in the novel, prepared by our own experience of time as a form of space, we learn that the way the man of the future has been able to reach us is not by an "impossible journey up the stream of time, but by a partial awakening, as it were, into eternity" (p. 181). From the perspective of eternity, time is a single expanse and thus the inspection of the past becomes possible. Ultimate consciousness, the birth of Absolute

Spirit, would of course mean not a partial but a total awakening into eternity, and this would involve the complete obliteration of time as we know it. But instead of ending with the incarnation of Absolute Spirit, the novel concludes with a lesser apocalypse, the death of mankind. The eighteenth men discover that a chain reaction among nearby stars is in the process of turning the sun into a nova and that mankind is doomed. Perhaps some form of intelligence elsewhere in the universe may awaken into the Absolute Spirit, but human history must be regarded as the story of a great purpose never fulfilled.

Can human history, two billion years of ultimately futile struggle and suffering, be justified? Stapledon's narrator repeatedly speaks of man's history as a kind of symphony in which various themes recur. Introducing the chronicle of human life on Neptune, for example, the narrator explains that his description of this final part of man's career will be brief.

Very much of it would be incomprehensible to terrestrials, and much of it repeats again and again, in the many Neptunian modes, themes that we have already observed in the Terrestrial or the Venerian movements of the human symphony. To appreciate fully the range and subtlety of the great living epic, we ought, no doubt, to dwell on its every movement with the same faithful care. But that is impossible to any human mind. We can but attend to significant phrases, here and there, and hope to capture some fragmentary hint of its vast intricate form.   (p.205)

Repeatedly, too, the various species of men have intimations that the fundamental principle behind existence is aesthetic, that history is to be conceived either as a kind of music or as a kind of tragic drama possessing a beauty "more difficult than the familiar beauty, but also more exquisite" (p.177). Faced with the imminent end of humanity, the eighteenth men are eventually able to see their fate "outlined clearly and beautifully against the cosmic background." Then, as the narrator who is himself one of the doomed explains, "we learned to contemplate the whole great saga of man as a completed work of art, and to admire it no less for its sudden and tragic end than for the promise in it which was not to be fulfilled" (p.237).

In its aestheticism *Last and First Men* is reminiscent of Nietzsche's dictum in *The Birth of Tragedy* that it is only as an aesthetic phenomenon that existence can be justified. What the aesthetic metaphor does, we should note, is finally to resolve the contradiction between sequence and simultaneity at the heart of the novel. Is succession the true nature of time? Or is time truly an expanse like space? The narrative has required us to experience both aspects of time as true. But now, by asking us to see history as analogous to music or to drama, the text introduces the idea of aesthetic time, that special realm in which succession can be contemplated as a whole or replayed at will. Moreover, the aesthetic metaphor results in the text, which is itself a tragic narrative, collapsing into its subject, becoming not only a telling of history but a model of history. In other words, the reader, having completed Stapledon's tragic novel, has not merely heard but in a sense experienced the tragic history of mankind.

The conception of aesthetic time obliterates normal ideas of history as irreversible succession. Nevertheless, at the novel's end, normal time reasserts itself in the vision of the vast unknown time of the cosmos, extending beyond man's little history in every direction. Man may be able to fly high enough to contemplate his own history as a whole, but "his knowledge of the great orb of things is but a fledgling's knowledge" (p.246). Man's history may be regarded as a symphony, and yet in relation to the vast music of cosmic existence humanity is merely a single theme. Whether that greater music is a completed symphony — indeed, whether it is music at all or merely noise "flecked now and then by shreds of significance" (p.234) — is impossible for any human mind to say.

Behind *Last and First Men* lies the fascination with and the fear of empty eons sweeping meaninglessly toward infinity. Stapledon's last men are space travelers as well as time travelers, and the narrator describes how on one voyage beyond the solar system the explorers are affected by their direct experience of vastness:

Throughout the voyage, which was the longest ever attempted they had encountered nothing whatever but two comets, and an occasional meteor. Some of the nearer constellations were seen with altered forms. One or two stars increased slightly in brightness; and the sun was reduced to being the most brilliant of stars. The aloof and changeless presence of the constellations seems to have crazed the voyagers. When at last the ship returned and berthed, there was a scene such as is seldom witnessed in our modern world. The crew flung open the ports and staggered blubbering into the arms of the crowd. It would never have been believed that members of our species could be so far reduced from the self-possession that is normal to us. Subsequently these poor human wrecks have shown an irrational phobia of the stars, and of all that is not human. (p. 218)

Stapledon loves vastness: the idea of vastness draws him into the ecstacy he expresses as the exhilaration of flying. But the love of vastness entails also the terror that his explorers discover. In employing the metaphor of human history as a completed tragedy, Stapledon has in effect drawn a magic circle around humanity, made a boundary between man and the void. In projecting human history as a work of art "outlined clearly and beautifully" against the vast eons of the cosmos, he has constructed an enclosure not unlike the enclosures characteristic of Jules Verne's fictions, a human space, safe and comforting, from which to gaze out at the infinite in fear and wonder together.

Like the tale of the future, the alternate-history narrative may also be understood as a logical extension of the time-travel fiction. In these stories time is conceived not as a single line but as an infinite number of branching lines, each representing a possible reality. What happens if a time traveler, interfering with the past, causes history to take a new course? In a sense, the traveler has not only journeyed backward in time but also laterally from one time stream to another. Murray Leinster's early and influential alternate-history story is significantly titled "Sidewise in Time" (1934). Alternate-history stories are sometimes quite explicit about their relationship to time travel. For example, Ward Moore's Bring the Jubilee (1955), which portrays a

world in which the South won the Civil War, concludes
with the invention of a time machine by which the protagonist, a historian, returns to observe the battle of
Gettysburg. His presence accidentally alters the course
of history and brings our own reality into being.

The alternate-history novel generally regards history
as a more or less arbitrary causal sequence. *Bring the
Jubilee* suggests that if matters had fallen out only
slightly otherwise at Gettysburg, the entire world
would be different. Much of the interest in such a fiction is related to the way the novel asks us to make
comparisons between its world and our own, recognizing the contingency of our lives, the way our view of
things is often determined by matters beyond our control. Behind the alternate history, then, lies once again
the characteristic science-fiction concern with free will
and determinism. Moreover, behind the alternate history is still another version of the Pascalian vertigo,
the dizzying vision of the infinite possibilities of times
that might have been.

The alternate history presents itself as a tangible,
substantial world as literal and real as our own. Nevertheless, the history it describes is conspicuously fictional. Philip K. Dick's *The Man in the High Castle*
(1962), which is perhaps the most interesting alternate-
history novel to date, exploits this contradiction in
order to question the very idea of tangible, objective
history. Is not all history in a sense a fiction? How can
we ever know anything about time except the fables
that we create? By raising such questions, Dick's novel
challenges the adequacy of any simplistic opposition
between ourselves and time. And his story becomes a

self-reflexive meditation not only upon the alternate history as a form but implicitly upon all science-fiction narratives concerned with the meaning of time.

The Man in the High Castle takes place in a world in which the Allies lost World War II and Germany and Japan partitioned the United States along with the rest of the globe. Most of the story is set in a curiously orientalized San Francisco. Pedicabs line the streets, instant tea dispensers hang on shop walls, people smoke marijuana cigarettes packaged with *haiku* or *waka* poems, and everyone consults the *I Ching*.

Robert Childan, the first character to whom we are introduced, is the proprietor of American Artistic Handcrafts Inc. Dealing in such items as Civil War handguns, Mickey Mouse watches, and antique posters, Childan sells objects that represent the prewar American culture. His clients are the Japanese who value such things for the "historicity" implicit in them and thus are willing to pay enormous prices for authentic American artifacts. At the start we accept Childan's objects at face value just as we accept the substantiality of Dick's fictional world at face value. But gradually the story questions our assumptions. The handguns in which Childan specializes turn out to be forgeries, and we realize that their value depends not so much upon any quality objectively inherent in them as upon belief. At the same time, the novel's world begins to turn fluid. Dick introduces a novel within a novel, *The Grasshopper Lies Heavy,* an alternate history that describes a world — similar to but not altogether identical with our own — in which the Allies won World War II. And at one point Mr. Tagomi, a Japanese trade official, finds himself mysteriously transported into a strange, rough San Francisco that we recognize as our own.

The novel's end, however, does not merely stretch the illusion of reality but ruptures it entirely. Here Dick at last produces Hawthorne Abendsen, the mysterious author of *The Grasshopper Lies Heavy.* Discovered by Juliana Frink, a young woman who has saved him from a Nazi assassination plot, Abendsen, who is supposed to live in a secret high castle, turns out to be an ordinary man living in an ordinary suburban house. On a hunch Juliana guesses correctly that Abendsen used the *I Ching* in composing his book. Calling for a copy of the *I Ching,* Juliana asks it why it wrote the novel and receives in answer the hexagram "Inner Truth."

> Raising his head, Hawthorne scrutinized her. He had now an almost savage expression. "It means, does it, that my book is true?"
> "Yes," she said.
> With anger he said, "Germany and Japan lost the war?"
> "Yes."[16]

Juliana's replies amount to a revelation that she and everyone else in the novel are merely fictions. What Dick has done is to violate the ground rule that the text should regard its own world as real. All along the text has been looking forward to some form of dramatic revelation that will come when the man in the high castle is found. But the insight when it comes turns out to be a strategically anticlimactic admission that the entire world of *The Man in the High Castle* is a fiction. Appropriately, Abendsen has turned out to be a nonentity, an absent figure as his name perhaps implies.

Like Childan's handguns, Dick's novel is forged history. But what after all is authenticity? Mr. Wyndam-Matson whose company manufactures the guns argues that the word "fake" means nothing because the word "authenticity" means nothing either: both terms simply refer to attitudes of the mind. And the novel as a whole repeatedly questions the value of authenticity as a concept. For example, dining with an elegant Japanese couple, Childan reflects upon the in-authentic nature of Japanese culture in general:

Even the *I Ching,* which they've forced down our throats; it's Chinese. Borrowed from way back when. Whom are they fooling? Themselves? Pilfer customs right and left, wear, eat, talk, walk, as for instance consuming with gusto baked potato served with sour cream and chives, old-fashioned American dish added to their haul. But nobody fooled, I can tell you; me least of all.   (pp. 111–112)

But Childan himself, who speaks and even sometimes thinks in the awkward cadences that the novel associates with the Japanese, is a cultural mongrel no less than his Japanese hosts, the Americanized Kasouras. The real distinction between the Kasouras and Childan, the novel suggests, is not to be made in terms of authenticity but in terms of balance. "The incredible Japanese sense of *Wabi,*" Childan thinks when he first sees their beautifully simple apartment, and then a moment later: "Balance. They are so close to the Tao, these two young Japanese" (pp. 104–105). The Kasouras are indeed balanced, secure in their self-possession, and this is the ground of their generosity and humanity. Childan is unbalanced and insecure, and this evidently is the source of the ugly fantasies of destructive domination to which he, like the Nazis he admires, is prone.

When Childan discovers that the antique guns in circulation are fakes, he fears lest the entire market in historical objects will collapse. Thus when a salesman appears with samples of original art jewelry, Childan is receptive: he immediately appreciates that the jewelry's value has nothing to do with authenticity. But will his Japanese clients accept the strange jewelry as art? In order to test the market, Childan gives one piece to Paul Kasouras, who is impressed. Indeed, Kasouras regards the pin as almost a magical object, identifying its value as *wu*, a Chinese term meaning among other things insight or wisdom. "It is balanced," he explains. "The forces within this piece are stabilized."

"The hands of the artificer," Paul said, "had wu, and allowed that wu to flow into this piece . . . By contemplating it, we gain more wu ourselves. We experience the tranquility associated not with art but with holy things. I recall a shrine in Hiroshima wherein a shinbone of some medieval saint could be examined. However, this is an artifact and that was a relic. This is alive in the now, whereas that merely *remained*. By this meditation, conducted by myself at great length since you were last here, I have come to identify the value which this has in opposition to historicity." (pp. 171–172)

Kasouras' statement also of course identifies the values that Dick's novel claims for itself: not historicity but balance and insight.

Absurdly solemn in their passion for objects such as Mickey Mouse watches and old comic books, Dick's Japanese are nevertheless presented as sane and balanced administrators who are genuinely concerned with the well-being of the peoples they rule. In fact their humorous and admirable qualities are related: both are associated with their distinctly oriental sense of history as represented in the novel by the *I Ching*. For this point of view, history is a series of unique changing moments, the character of each moment being the product of the auspicious or inauspicious configuration of events at the instant. Every life, every object, is bound up with every other in the complex pattern of the moment, and thus everything is worthy of consideration and respect. The law that underlies the movement of history is the principle of balance: the universe continually seeks a harmonious state of balance, seeks to come to rest in the Tao. Right action is always action in accord with the Tao; for an individual or society to become unbalanced, to move away from the Tao, is ominous.

Opposed to the humane Japanese are the Nazis. In victory the Nazis have not only pressed their campaign for the extermination of the Jews, they have also driven the Slavs out of Europe and have attempted to eradicate the entire black population of Africa. But the Nazis also have achieved technological triumphs far beyond the Japanese's capabilities, developing interplanetary travel and beginning the colonization of the solar system. Again, both their monstrous and their impressive qualities are related to their vision of the nature of things and particularly to their sense of history. Blind to particularities, their view is, as one character says, "cosmic." They live in a world of abstractions, seeing through the here and now "into the vast black deep beyond, the unchanging." The only relationship between themselves and the outside world that they can imagine is a contest for total domination: "They want to be the agents, not the victims of history." The Nazis, we can note, are pursuing exactly the same dream of godlike power, of endless expansion into the infinite, that characterizes so much science fiction. And in that Western, alienated vision the novel finds the source of both accomplishment and madness. Appropriately, the plot revolves around an apocalyptic Nazi scheme for the total annihilation of the Japanese in a sneak atomic attack.

The Japanese in *The Man in the High Castle* do not merely inhabit a different part of the globe from the Nazis, they inhabit a different reality. Which reality is authentic? Which is true? In structure as well as in moral judgment, the novel confirms the oriental view, the commitment to the reality of the particular and the vision of history as a process of mutual implication. Dick's characters are conspicuously "particular," especially when seen in the context of the abstract representative figures usual in science fiction. Moreover, there is no central consciousness in the novel, no one character who imposes his will upon the story and compels us to see it in his terms. Rather, the narrative skips from consciousness to consciousness, leaving the reader to discover the hidden pattern, the "moment" in which all the lives in the book are bound together. Reading the novel then becomes analogous to consulting the *I Ching:* gradually the pattern takes shape until we attain the truth of the hexagram that represents the moment. The process is a passage from ignorance to insight, a movement inward from the misleading surface – the novel abounds in secret schemes and disguised figures – to the hidden essence of things. And yet even as the novel confirms the oriental vision of reality as true, it reminds us that it itself is only a fiction. "Reality," "authenticity," "historicity" – these are all as much matters of the collective imagination as of objective fact. Once again, the proper issue is not truth but balance, wisdom.

We can observe now that *The Man in the High Castle* may be understood as analogous in some respects to Lem's *Solaris. Solaris* transforms problems of cosmology into problems of epistemology, and in the process it subverts or at least renders problematic the very opposition between the human and the nonhuman that constitutes the text. As Knights of the Holy Contact, do we really encounter anything but images of ourselves, the "phi creatures" drawn from our own deepest patterns of thought? Looking into the void, which is not after all truly a void but a universe replete with otherness, can we ever really see anything but our own faces? Similarly, *The Man in the High Castle* transforms problems of eschatology, or purpose in history, into problems of epistemology. Can we really regard time as something outside ourselves, an alien antagonist to be conquered or a dominion to be appro-

priated and ruled? Looking into the dark abysm of
time, which is not after all really an abysm or any
other kind of spatial realm, do we not also discover a
face that is our own?

Having considered the future history and the alternate
history, let us return to the time-travel narrative
proper. Brian Aldiss' *Cryptozoic* (1967), in which time
travel is accomplished by taking a mind-altering drug,
suggests the movement toward interiorization characteristic of "late" texts. Does time in fact run
backwards? Are our lives actually journeys toward
rather than away from the womb? *Cryptozoic* poses
this bizarre possibility, playing with its metaphorical
implications and exploring the relationship between
consciousness and time. Even richer than *Cryptozoic*,
however, is J. G. Ballard's *The Drowned World* (1962) in
which the idea of time travel is employed purely as a
metaphor. *The Drowned World,* moreover, not only
provides an example of emphatic interiorization but
also suggests the way that fictions of time are drawn
by the force of a kind of inner linguistic gravity until
they collapse into fictions of space. This tendency may
be understood as the reciprocal of that through which
spatially conceived narratives such as *Journey to the
Centre of the Earth* or *The War of the Worlds* expand
toward a concern with time.
　　Like *The Time Machine,* to which the text explicitly
alludes, *The Drowned World* portrays a devolving
world, a planet collapsing back into primeval chaos.
Here, however, devolution is not the result of gradual
entropic decline but a sudden climatic change brought

about by solar instability. Over a period of a few decades the earth has become fiercely hot and the polar icecaps have begun to melt, raising global water levels and transforming Europe into a system of lagoons. Moreover, higher levels of radioactivity resulting from the dispersal of the ionosphere have led to drastic increases in the rate of mutation. Archaic plant and animal forms — fern trees and giant lizards — have reappeared and are fast taking over the world. The entire planet has been launched on what is in effect a geological and biological journey backward in time toward the Mesozoic.

As one might expect in a text in which the idea of time travel is located in the landscape, directionality acquires temporal as well as spatial significance. Vastly reduced in numbers as a result of a general decline in mammalian fertility — all the higher forms of life are dying off — mankind has retreated to the still habitable region of Camp Byrd within the arctic circle. In the north lies the future; in the south are the steaming jungles and lagoons of the distant, prehuman past. And yet from another point of view the north represents the past, for ultimately even the pole must become uninhabitable: humanity, at least in its present form, is doomed. A broken compass — the calibrated ring has rotated 180 degrees so that the instrument perversely points south — figures prominently, indicating the direction in which the magnetic currents of nature now flow. Should one yield to these currents or struggle against them? Concerned with a mapping and survey expedition that is traveling — significantly — from south to north, the initial direction of the narrative is

TIME

opposed to the current. At the end, however, the direction changes as Robert Kerans, a biologist whose task is to catalogue the new forms of life, abandons the expedition and sets off on a solitary journey south.

Time in this fiction is not only located in the external world, it is also something inscribed within. At work for months in the melting, metamorphosing city of London — neither north nor south, no longer inhabited but not yet totally claimed by jungle and lagoon, London is an intermediate locale, a "zone of transit" — Kerans and other members of the expedition have begun to exhibit a pronounced lassitude and introversion. Their symptoms recall "the slackening metabolism and biological withdrawal of all animal forms about to undergo a major metamorphosis."[17] A few have also begun to experience exhausting hypnotic dreams. Dominated by a great booming sun and by the sound of reptiles baying in the lagoon, the dreams seem to express an urge to melt into the formlessness of the primitive watery environment. These are not, however, normal dreams but ancient organic memories that are being activated by the rising temperature and humidity, releasing instincts that have lain dormant for millennia.

As Alan Bodkin, who is Kerans' colleague in the biological arm of the expedition, explains, the trace of the evolutionary past is written in every human chromosome and gene.

Each one of us is as old as the entire biological kingdom, and our bloodstreams are tributaries of the great sea of its total memory. The uterine odyssey of the growing foetus recapitulates the entire evolutionary past, and its central nervous system is a coded time-scale, each nexus of neurons and each spinal level marking a symbolic station, a unit of neuronic time.

In response to the earth's backward journey in geophysical time, Bodkin suggests, man is changing psychically. The process can be understood as a "uterine odyssey" in reverse. The "amniotic corridor" is reentered and the individual begins a journey backward in "spinal and archaeopsychic time" in which the unconscious mind takes on the landscape of successively earlier epochs, "each with a distinct geological terrain, its own unique flora and fauna, as recognizable to anyone else as they would be to a traveller in a Wellsian time machine. Except that this is no scenic railway, but a total reorientation of the personality." Bodkin warns that "if we let these buried phantoms master us as they reappear we'll be swept back helplessly in the flood-tide like pieces of flotsam" (pp. 43–44).

The drowned world of the title, then, refers not merely to the watery world of the exterior landscape, but also to the submarine regions of the psyche, the amniotic oceans of the biological past. Moreover, as both the title and Bodkin's warning imply, the descent into the drowned world is a slide into unconsciousness and death. In "The Pool of Thanatos," a chapter that makes explicit the connection between the drowned world and death, Kerans descends into the lagoon to explore the sunken London Planetarium. Inside the building his airhose becomes snarled and he begins to

130

suffocate, imagining as he slips into oblivion that the
sparkling cracks in the dome represent the ancient
constellations of a primeval epoch. Later Kerans
wonders whether he did not perhaps mean to snarl his
hose. Was he unconsciously accepting the logic of the
earth's devolution and willingly sinking into death?
Mysterious processes are at work within him, and he is
no longer the master of his own intentions. The image
of the sunken planetarium in this episode also makes
explicit the way the familiar science-fiction icon of the
starry infinite has been transferred to a watery world
located below and within rather than above and outside. As in *Solaris* where the image of the alien ocean
draws upon the sea's traditional attributes of mystery
and vastness, so here the rising waters of the devolving
planet can be understood as another version of the incomprehensible, shapeless infinite, the void of the
prehuman. In *The Drowned World,* however, the
watery void is also part of ourselves.

Form and formlessness, life and death — these are
the terms at play in the narrative. In the opening
phases of the story the struggle between life and death
centers on the question of whether Kerans will return
north with Colonel Riggs or remain in the sunken city
with Beatrice Dahl. Riggs, the "buoyant" leader of the
expedition, and Beatrice, the beautiful, indolent
woman with whom Kerans has established a desultory
liaison, are antithetical figures. Always scrubbed and
clean-shaven, Riggs is the sort of brisk, intelligent
military man who has little patience with obscure
urges. He epitomizes the impulse toward order implicit
in a mission devoted to mapping and cataloguing.

Beatrice, on the other hand, who is first described as a "sleeping python," is a native of the lagoon. An aura of decadence clings to her and to her opulent penthouse, stocked with reserves of frozen pâté de foie gras and filet mignon, where she has been holding out for years against the rising heat and water. In particular the narrative calls our attention to two paintings in her apartment, images respectively of grotesque living death and agonized deadly life. The first is a Delvaux in which "ashen-faced women danced naked to the waist with dandified skeletons against a spectral bone-like landscape." The second is a Max Ernst image of the sun in which a "self-devouring phantasmagoric" jungle "screamed silently to itself, like the sump of some insane unconscious" (p. 29).

To remain in London with the temperature and water level still rising seems perverse and suicidal. As Kerans says when Beatrice proposes that he stay, "You realize that if we let Riggs go without us we don't merely leave here later. We *stay*" (p. 29). The figure of Lieutenant Hardman also helps to establish the significance of staying. A solitary and quiet man even in normal circumstances, Hardman, who has been experiencing the hypnotic dreams for months, has lapsed into complete torpor and is now confined to the sickbay. But when he learns that Riggs is pulling out, Hardman has a sudden surge of strength and runs away. A helicopter search discovers him heading, madly, south. With maniacal energy the man eludes capture and disappears into the jungles and lagoons, plunging toward the fierce sun and certain death.

Riggs departs. Kerans, Bodkin, and Beatrice remain,

132

each living in his own quarters, each pursuing his
solitary pathway through the "time jungles" of the unconscious. And then Strangman, a scavenger combing
the abandoned cities, arrives. With his crew of brutal,
illiterate blacks and his weird train of alligators,
Strangman is an ominous figure. Kerans associates him
with the tuxedoed skeletons of the Delvaux painting,
and when Strangman displays his loot, Kerans remarks
that the collected objects, gathered from all the cities
of Europe, are like bones. In a remarkable feat of
engineering, Strangman and his crew drain the lagoon
in order to make the sunken buildings accessible. To
Kerans, however, the city's exposure is an abomination,
the exhumation of a corrupted body.

Everything was covered with a fine coating of silt, smother-
ing whatever grace and character had once distinguished
the streets, so that the entire city seemed to Kerans to have
been resurrected from its own sewers. Were the Day of
Judgment to come, the armies of the dead would probably
rise clothed in the same filthy mantle. (p. 125)

Furthermore, Kerans understands now that he cannot
do without the primeval landscape; the lagoon fulfills
a "complex of neuronic needs" that have become
essential to his being. By remaining in London he has
committed himself to a form of time travel. But now,
with the rotting city exposed in the middle of the
jungle, he feels "like a man marooned in a time sea,
hemmed in by the shifting planes of dissonant realities
millions of years apart" (p. 127).

Repulsive and dangerous, Strangman is the pivotal

figure in the narrative. Through him the text urges us
to revalue the attempt, represented also by Riggs and
the polar colony, to preserve the old order. The
civilization of Europe is dead. Mankind itself, in its old
form, is dead. How long can even Camp Byrd hold out
against the changing planet? Why attempt to preserve
a corpse, to raise rotting bones from the grave? Does
the devolving planet leave any option for life or only a
choice between two forms of death, the one represented by the dancing bones of the Delvaux and the
other by the Max Ernst with its mad, self-devouring
jungle?

A sense of fate, a feeling that obscure forces are
working toward a necessary conclusion, presses upon
the narrative. Referred to repeatedly, the Delvaux and
Ernst paintings, grotesque visions that are rapidly being
realized at the literal level of the story, develop
oracular status. The south-pointing compass is also
oracular, and again and again characters appear to be
acting from motives that they themselves barely comprehend and over which they have diminishing control.
The text also attempts to confirm the sense of fate by
suggesting that through the particular characters archetypal mythic roles are being fulfilled. Strangman
with his chalk-white face and his attendant crocodiles
is a kind of voodoo god of death. Indeed, at one point
he halfhumorously confides to Kerans that his men
fear him because they think he is dead. Beatrice, too,
gathers an aura of quasi-divinity – she is, variously, a
Venus returning to the sea and a Minerva marrying
Neptune – that activates the allusion to Dante's mistress latent in her name. All of these elements of

course point ultimately to the fact of the changing planet, to the fact that geological and biological forces are working toward a conclusion.

The story comes to a crisis when Bodkin, acting out of the same obscure need for the lagoon that Kerans feels, attempts to reflood the city. Bodkin is promptly shot, and Kerans is handed over to the blacks, strapped to a throne, beaten, covered with refuse, and exposed for several days to the sun. Beginning as an act of reprisal, the torture of Kerans turns into a primitive rite of exorcism in which Strangman's men, identifying the biologist with the sea that they hate and fear, attempt through him to demonstrate their power over the rising waters. In a suggestive action that looks forward both to his reflooding of the city and to his ultimate journey south, Kerans stoically accepts the sacrificial role of Neptune in which he has been cast by circumstances. Somehow he manages to survive the beating and exposure. He escapes from Strangman, returns to his suite at the Ritz Hotel to find that it has been sacked, and then realizes that he must leave the city and go south.

His time there had outlived itself, and the air-sealed suite with its constant temperature and humidity, its supplies of fuel and food, were nothing more than an encapsulated form of his previous environment, to which he had clung like a reluctant embryo to its yolk sac ... Now he would have to go forward. Both the past, represented by Riggs, and the present contained within the demolished penthouse, no longer offered a viable existence. His commitment to the future, so far one of choice and plagued by so many doubts and hesitations, was now absolute. (pp. 144–145)

135

As the metaphor of the embryo suggests, Kerans' departure now represents a form of life – the time of languid inaction has been a period of gestation – and a necessary embracing of an uncertain and fluid future.

Attempting to flee with Beatrice on a homemade raft, Kerans is stopped by Strangman, who is about to kill him when Colonel Riggs reappears. Kerans assumes that Riggs will arrest Strangman and reflood the lagoon: "Have you been down to those streets; they're obscene and hideous! It's a nightmare world that's dead and finished" (p. 156). But Riggs refuses, pointing out that the reclamation of land is a major priority of the government at Camp Byrd. Legally, Strangman was entitled to kill Bodkin for interfering, and Riggs himself will do the same if anyone else tries to repeat Bodkin's attempt. The gulf between Kerans and Riggs is absolute. From Riggs's point of view, Kerans is mad, out of touch with reality. From Kerans' point of view, Riggs is the madman, a ghostly relic of a past that no longer exists: "It was Riggs and not himself, who was the time-traveller" (p. 155). That night Kerans blasts the dam holding back the water and the future and, like Hardman before him, disappears into the jungle.

Foreshadowed by his earlier descent to the sunken planetarium, Kerans' voyage down the curve of the devolving planet toward the teeming chaos of the equator is at the same time an embracing of life, a quest for the magical point of life's origin in the hot womb of nature, and a suicidal flight toward death. It represents an acceptance of the future and of the archaic past toward which the future is moving. Like Axel's and Lidenbrock's subterranean journey, Kerans' voyage is a quest for the center, the mystical locale at which extremes meet and opposites become identical. Moreover, as in Verne's narrative, the center – here the equator – is opposed to the pole, Camp Byrd, the boundary region at the farthest verge of nature's sphere. In Verne, the attainment of the center, the reaching of the hot, fluid core of the globe, would mean the absolute possession of nature, the achievement of a zone in which all being would be immediately present. In Ballard, too, the goal is a magical zone in which the distinction between man and nature, between Kerans' tortured consciousness and the abyss of the infinite that is at once inside and outside mankind, ceases to exist.

Throughout Ballard's narrative – in, for example, the image of the sunken planetarium as "an immense submarine temple" and in the association of Beatrice with Dante's guide to the realms of transcendence – there have been hints of the essentially religious nature of the goal toward which the fiction has been moving. Appropriately, Kerans' journey, a quest for a "spectral grail" (p. 45) first announced by the south-pointing compass and then given form in the visionary dreams of the booming sun, is a kind of holy pilgrimage. Moving steadily southward, the traveler encounters "what seemed to be the remains of a small temple" where he finds Hardman, emaciated, diseased, and insane, his eyesight almost completely gone as a result of corneal cancers produced by staring at the sun. Hardman and his fate suggest the terrible future that lies ahead for Kerans. But madness, as we know, may be divine, and blindness may imply spiritual sight; as the setting in the temple suggests, Hardman need not be seen simply as a figure of horror.

Kerans feeds the dying man and attends to his eyes. He is not surprised when Hardman, his strength revived, vanishes into the jungle. Moving on himself, plunging deeper and deeper into the jungles of the past, Kerans attempts to maintain some hold on normal time by recording the passage of days on his belt, and he attempts, too, to hold in his mind as clearly and as long as he can the memory of Beatrice. "So he left the lagoon and entered the jungle again, within a few days he was completely lost, following the lagoons southward through the increasing rain and heat, attacked by alligators and giant bats, a second Adam searching for the forgotten paradises of the reborn sun" (p. 171). Delicately recapitulating the entire narrative, the fiction concludes appropriately on a note of continuing quest as Kerans presses toward the mystical locale that is at once a place and a time, an ultimate point of origin and a final point of return.

MACHINE

Wells's time machine is a positive image, a sign of the power of reason expressed through science. But the machine in this novel also becomes a negative image both in the Morlock underworld of thudding machines and in the suggestion of history as a diabolical mechanism. The role of machines in science fiction is double. Machines typically mediate between the human and the nonhuman, serving as the agency through which man explores and protects himself from the cosmos. But at the same time, as versions of the nonhuman, machines may represent a threat to humane values.

Behind the positive attitudes toward machines in science fiction ultimately lies the mechanistic world view that emerged in the seventeenth and eighteenth centuries. Not only did the cosmos come to be viewed as a machine, an enormous piece of celestial clockwork, but living bodies as well were regarded as automata. Recall Thomas Hobbes's comparison of the state to a man and man to a machine at the start of *Leviathan* (1651): "For what is the *Heart* but a *Spring;* and the *Nerves* but so many *Strings;* and the *Joynts* but so many *Wheeles,* giving motion to the whole Body, such as was intended by the Artificer?"[1] There was commonly a sense of triumph in such applications of the mechanical metaphor to natural processes – to compare the cosmos or even humanity to machines was to say that the world was explicable – and in the course of the eighteenth century the mechanistic explanation of nature hardened into dogma.

The mechanistic world view was one of the factors

that made possible the triumph of the industrial revolution in the first half of the nineteenth century. Powerfully impressed by the new factories and railroads, the early nineteenth century was aware of itself as an age of machines. "Were we required to characterise this age of ours by any single epithet," Thomas Carlyle wrote in 1829, "we should be tempted to call it, not an Heroical, Devotional, Philosophical, or Moral Age, but, above all others, the Mechanical Age."[2]

Carlyle was ambivalent about machines — on the one hand he admired their power, and on the other he distrusted the false application of mechanistic principles to organic processes — and the age was equally ambivalent. The romantic movement of the turn of the century can be understood as a protest against the mechanistic world view, and it was in this period that the familiar opposition between the mechanical and the organic, between the dark, satanic mills and the beauty of the green and pleasant land, became fully formed. More and more, as the process of industrialization advanced, the attitude of the nineteenth century shifted from delight in machines as the servants of man to fear of them as destroyers of life. For John Ruskin, to cite perhaps the most influential Victorian critic of industrialization, the machine became an almost apocalyptic image of evil, a tangible symbol of the desecration of a sacramental world. Ruskin saw the industrial system as the agent of dehumanization, and his work took the form of an evangelical crusade against machines in the name of the human: "Men were not intended to work with the accuracy of tools, to be precise and perfect in all their actions. If you will have that precision out of them, and make their fingers measure degrees like cog-wheels, and their arms strike curves like compasses, you must unhumanize them. All the energy of their spirits must be given to make cogs and compasses of themselves."[3]

Ruskin traced nineteenth-century social unrest to the enslavement that the industrial system involved, and he is often cited in connection with Karl Marx's contemporaneous social analysis. For Marx the problem lay not in mechanization as such but in private ownership of the means of production. Nevertheless, Marx and Ruskin shared the same basic perception of the unsatisfactory position of the worker in the nineteenth-century industrial system. In Marx's analysis — it is from Marx that the term "alienation" has come into general currency — the worker comes to face his own product as an independent power, an alien being: "The *alienation* of the worker in his product means not only that his labour becomes an object, assumes an *external* existence, but that it exists independently, *outside himself,* and alien to him, and that it stands opposed to him as an autonomous power. The life which he has given to the object sets itself against him as an alien and hostile force."[4]

Marx's discussion of alientated labor sounds almost like a prescription for science fiction, but this should not be wholly surprising. As a genre science fiction comes into being not only as a medium for expression of the feeling of separation from physical nature, the alienated senses both of space and of time, but also for expression of the feeling of social disconnection that accompanied urbanization and industrialization.

ALIEN ENCOUNTERS

In part the appearance of science fiction as a genre
may be understood directly in relation to the industrial
revolution and the ambivalence with which it was
received. Although the early literary response to the
new world of technology was considerable, it is striking that the major writers of the first two thirds of the
nineteenth century who are centrally concerned with
machines tend, with the notable exception of Dickens,
to be essayists and social critics rather than novelists.
In science fiction writers found a form of fiction suited
for dealing with the new circumstances of life in a
world shaped and populated by machines as well as by
men.

Like the epic to which its subtitle alludes, Stanley
Kubrick's and Arthur C. Clarke's film *2001: A Space
Odyssey* (1969) is dominated by the idea of the
journey. Tracing mankind's history from the subhuman
apes to the superhuman starchild, the film enacts a
four-million-year evolutionary voyage that is also a
journey into space. The spatial odyssey commences
with the bone that is hurled triumphantly into the air
and that then, in an astonishing filmic ellipsis that includes all of human history, becomes the orbiting
satellite. Once initiated, the journey moves continuously outward – Dr. Floyd journeys to the space station and then on to the moon; the Jupiter ship
journeys into the outer solar system; Bowman journeys
beyond the solar system entirely – and this steady outward movement helps to provide a sense of narrative
direction for the film. Closure is achieved when the
starchild returns to earth, breaking the pattern of out-

ward movement and completing mankind's voyage. Floating freely toward earth, the starchild is a version of Odysseus, lord of Ithaca, returning home at last.

The formal pattern of the journey finds its stylistic counterpart in the film's concentration on movement. Planets and satellites, natural and artificial, swing in arcs of changing illumination as their positions vary with respect to the sun; space vessels course silently toward and away from ports that are themselves in motion; within the vessels centrifuges spin, providing artificial gravity; and in control rooms computer display screens clicking new images from second to second graphically model the complex spatial relations between mutually moving bodies. In this world, still-ness of any kind is an illusion: everything is in process, movement, transformation. The Jupiter ship, floating in apparent calm against the background of the stars, is in fact hurtling through space at enormous speed. Likewise, the apparent calm of the vault that is HAL's brain and consciousness disguises the frenetic activity of the millions of microcurrents that constitute the computer's terror. Mankind itself, apparently a stable form, is of course also in evolutionary motion, just as the physical universe is in a process of continual un-seen metamorphosis, as the images of the Big Bang and of galactic and stellar condensations in the final, semiabstract segment of the film remind us.[5]

Structuring and containing the dynamic world of the film is the fundamental opposition between the finitude of the human and the infinitude of the non-human. The alien beauty of space is omnipresent, either dwelt upon directly as in the sequences of astronomical bodies in movement or presented indirectly as immanent in the curved, centrifugal spaces of the orbiting station and of the Jupiter ship's living quarters. The weightless environment in which every human movement becomes a deliberate and studied action — recall, for instance, the stewardesses in the Orion and Aries vessels — also keeps us continuously aware of our immersion in the void. Both literally and metaphorically, the film's background is infinity. In the foreground are the elaborate machines that mediate between man and infinity. Repeatedly, views of space are framed in windows, visors, and ports, and more expansive shots of space are generally composed with a moving vehicle of some sort in the middle distance, providing a sense of depth and relationship.

Machines are the agency through which mankind moves toward the infinite. Conversely, the mysterious black slabs are the agency through which the infinite moves toward mankind. Apparently immobile, the featureless black slab that manifests itself to the apes in "The Dawn of Man" contains the emptiness of space: like Wells's Martians, the slab embodies the void. In its rectilinear form, however, the slab contrasts both with the rounded natural forms of space, the spinning globes of planets and moons, and with the weathered organic forms of earth among which it is discovered. Not only a version of the infinite but also an artifact, the slab is apprehended as a kind of transcendent machine. Unmoved mover of the fable, the slab in its mysterious action upon the apes initiates an activity that is appropriately reciprocal to its own: in the primeval bone technology is born and the human movement toward the infinite is begun.

MACHINE

The birth of technology is also the birth of man.
Defining man as a tool-using animal, *2001* implies both
that mankind was in effect created by a machine and
that his evolutionary history is inseparable from the
evolutionary history of his machines. The apes are
presented as aggressive, frustrated pack animals,
vulnerable to predators such as the leopard and only
marginally successful in the Pleistocene competition
for food because of their lack of natural weapons.
Significantly, the first tool is also the first weapon. Us-
ing the bone as a cudgel to bring down their prey, the
apes become meat eaters, and, directing the weapon
against a rival pack, they also become successful war-
makers. Later scenes establish the continuity between
primeval and modern times. The Jupiter ship, elon-
gated and knobby, is in a sense no more than an elaborate bone, and the design of the episode in which the
space-suited Americans examine the slab on the moon
explicitly recalls the apes gathering about the original
slab. Most important, as the hints of international ten-
sions suggest, mankind is still a frustrated and aggressive pack animal.

Our first images of the modern world, however, emphasize the differences within the human continuity.
With the "Blue Danube" controlling our aesthetic
response — Strauss's waltz here suggests elegance and
culture — we are introduced to a civilization of wonderful dancing machines as we watch the Orion shuttle
gracefully match its movements to those of the
rotating space station. The world suggested by this
crucial sequence is above all a place of exquisite
beauty, and the machines into which the primeval
bone has evolved are the signs of the creative power

through which mankind has transformed the realm of near space into a kind of technological pastoral.

Contrasted with the black of space and the blue swirls of the earth below, the Orion shuttle and the wheeling station are starkly white, a color that carries forward the bone's whiteness but that here suggests purity and rationality. It also suggests the sterility of the inorganic, but we should not miss the hints of sexuality implicit in the image of the shuttle penetrating the station and, later, in the image of the Clavius moonbase slowly opening to receive the Aries shuttle. Like the control room, the "brain" of the Aries shuttle, and like HAL's memory vault, the womblike cavern of the Clavius airlock is suffused with an organic red light. And in the image of the Aries descending, its observation ports glowing like eyes and its articulated struts extending beneath it like feet, we have the first emphatic suggestion of machines acquiring independent life, a movement that climaxes in HAL.

The boundary between the organic and the inorganic is transgressed from the opposite direction as well; as machines are coming alive, so men are becoming more like machines. Sexuality is conspicuously absent from the film's sterile human world. Indeed, emotion itself is absent, not so much suppressed as simply gone. Recall Dr. Floyd's mechanically hearty visiphone conversation with his daughter or Bowman vacantly listening to his parents' prerecorded birthday greetings. As these episodes suggest, human bonds, even the primary bond between parent and child, have become tenuous. Again and again, the camera dwells upon disconnected figures – Dr. Floyd and the stewardess sitting on opposite sides of the large elevator that opens on the space station's deck, Bowman and Poole in the living quarters of the Jupiter ship – and the human figures are often separated from each other both physically and psychologically by the machines that they have come to resemble.

Just as the formal and thematic idea of the journey penetrates the film's style in the concentration on movement, so the concern with the natural versus the artificial is reflected in the compositional emphasis on rounded versus rectilinear forms. Roundedness is introduced in the film's opening image of the sun rising over the earth as seen from the moon. Rectilinearity is established in the image of the slab. Again and again, after "The Dawn of Man," shots are composed in terms of the contrast between rounded and rectilinear forms, as when Dr. Floyd is shown seated before the square of the visiphone talking to his daughter while in the background, seen through a huge rectangular window, the earth's ball rolls by. Interior spaces, too, tend to be conspicuously rectilinear – the docking port of the round space station, the conference room at Clavius, HAL's memory vault – or conspicuously rounded in the manner of the Jupiter ship's centrifugal chamber. Appropriately, machines are as likely to possess rounded as rectilinear forms. (Vehicles tend to be rounded, display screens rectangular or square.) Rather than being used to identify the artificial or the natural, the contrasted compositional forms serve, once their meaning has been established, to preserve the abstract idea of the natural versus the artificial as a category of perception.

ALIEN ENCOUNTERS

Much of *2001's* drama derives from the progressive erasure of the boundary between the natural and the artificial, the organic and the inorganic, and from the cinematic exploration of the significance of the dangerous confusions that result. Our initial perception of the beauty of the realm of dancing space machines is soon qualified by the satiric treatment of the impersonal, commercialized world of the Hilton-operated space station and of such mechanized figures as Dr. Floyd, who is consistently oblivious to the beauties of space that surround him. As the lyric yields to the satiric, so the satiric in turn gradually becomes horrific. Beginning with the descending Aries shuttle's glowing "eyes" and climaxing in the long Jupiter ship with its globular "head," articulated vertebrae, and brood of two-handed pods, the machines more and more come to resemble grotesque, malevolent creatures. The potential for confrontation between man and machine is realized in the open warfare between HAL and the astronauts. Here, in the contrast between the unfeeling, mechanical deaths of the three hibernating astronauts and the extended pathos of HAL's own "death," the transposition of man and machine reaches its furthest point. The unconscious astronauts are merely switched off – "Life Functions Terminated," the readout screen announces when they have died – whereas HAL succumbs in genuinely affecting agony, repeating over and over that he feels afraid.

The issue at stake in the struggle is which form of life is fittest to survive in space. At this point the film begins to dwell upon the vulnerable, organic nature of man. Poole dies of asphyxiation, his airhose severed by

148

the pod under HAL's control, and Bowman, attempting to reenter the ship after retrieving Poole's body, must expose himself momentarily to the vacuum. Dominating the soundtrack whenever Poole or Bowman wears a spacesuit are the amplified sounds of human breathing, which remind us not only of the astronauts' vulnerability but that space is always a hostile environment, one in which they cannot endure without elaborate protection. On the other hand, HAL and the ship that is, in effect, his body are very much in their proper environment, a fact that makes Bowman's ultimate defeat of the computer all the more remarkable.

The film's last segment, "Jupiter and Beyond the Infinite," recapitulates earlier themes in a new key. Floating in the vicinity of Jupiter, Bowman's pod falls toward one of the mysterious slabs and then, in a visual realization of the abstract idea of a journey, we are suddenly speeding through a seemingly endless corridor of rectangular forms. Eventually the mechanical shapes of the corridor yield to rounded, natural forms, and the journey in space becomes also a journey in time as we see exploding and then slowly swirling images that suggest the creation of the universe in the Big Bang and the condensation of galaxies and stars. Finally, we find ourselves cruising above deserted, oddly colored landscapes that in their emptiness recall the opening views of the barren landscape of the primeval apes. Throughout the strange journey, direct views of unearthly forms are intercut with images of Bowman's visored face and then with hugely magnified closeups of his watching eye. Repeatedly, *2001* has shown us the world through windows and visors. Equally important, it has suggested varieties of mechanical seeing: the visiphone picture of Dr. Floyd's daughter, the computer display projections on navigation screens, HAL's fisheye lens view of the world. In other words, the film has suggested that seeing itself, which it identifies with consciousness, has come to be a mechanically mediated activity. Now, however, in the extreme closeups of Bowman's hyperbolically organic eye responding directly to the extraordinary images before it, the film suggests the possibility of unmediated vision, of direct consciousness of the universe.

Suddenly the universe is gone. Without warning, the film cuts from the closeup of Bowman's eye to the stylized and conspicuously windowless eighteenth-century bedroom with the pod sitting incongruously in the middle of the floor. From hints of unmediated vision the film has jumped to the opposite extreme, total enclosure and complete lack of access to the outside world. The room is startling precisely because it is so unexpectedly human, and the presence of the pod, a vehicle designed for the exploration of space, emphasizes the shock of the domestic. As in *Solaris* where enclosed spaces such as the library suggest man's imprisonment in his own mind, so here the idea of human imprisonment in human culture is evident.

The sequence that follows, in which Bowman discovers successively older versions of himself, develops the inwardness implicit in the setting, suggesting a drama of self-discovery. Step by step the paraphrenalia of space and the mechanical way of life they represent are shed – the film implicitly defines this movement as a development from youthful barbarism to mature civilization – until the narrative comes to a momentary rest in the image of Bowman as a white-haired gentleman eating a formal dinner that in its civilized elegance contrasts sharply with the processed, artificial meals prominent in the film's middle sections. Reaching across the table, Bowman accidentally knocks over a crystal wineglass, a symbol of civilization. As the breaking of the wineglass suggests, this stage of development, too, will be left behind. Again we hear heavy breathing sounds and the camera pans upward to reveal a last, decrepit version of the astronaut, lying in bed. Man himself is evidently coming to an end. At the bed's foot stands the last of the slabs, and a glowing mist containing the image of a fetus replaces the ancient man. Under the aegis of the slab mankind was created and now, again under the slab's aegis, something new has been created in mankind's place. Suddenly the enclosing, windowless room disappears and we are in open space again, the rolling images of the moon and the earth filling the screen. The effect is one of exhilaration, of release into freedom. Gradually the fetus, enclosed only in a globe of mist, floats into view, its bright eyes recalling the earlier hints of unmediated consciousness, and the film ends with the starchild staring enigmatically into the audience.

The full meaning of the starchild, like that of the slabs, lies precisely in its indeterminacy. Nevertheless, we can note that from the story of the infant Moses to Shakespeare's Marina the image of the mysterious newborn child arriving from the sea has been a powerful romance motif, suggesting the appearance of a new force that will fundamentally alter the nature of things. Clearly an organic being and yet one that can move in space without artifice, the starchild resolves the opposition between man and machine that has occupied the narrative foreground. Structurally speaking, the round starchild also resolves the anomaly of the slabs, providing a transcendent version of the organic that balances their transcendent version of the rectilinear and artificial. Finally, however, the starchild is merely an empty sign pointing toward the birth of a power that in its transcendence of all earthly limitations can be identified with infinity. The entire narrative, beginning with the primeval bone hurled into the air, has been an enactment of mankind's journey toward the infinite. In the end, man's quest neither succeeds nor fails: instead of conquering the infinite, he becomes the infinite.

Beginning as tools, agents through which man can explore and humanize the cosmos, the machines in *2001* gradually develop independence and become the alien. Indeed, Kubrick's machines, their skeletal limbs extended and their eyes glowing, at times even look like the familiar movie monsters from outer space. If mankind is Odysseus, then HAL with his single red eye is the monster Cyclops whom Odysseus must defeat in order to return home.

2001 implies the range of machines in science fiction. At one pole machines may be purely human instruments, as they are in Verne; at another they become indistinguishable from aliens. Thus there arises a subcategory of stories in which — as in Lem's *The Invincible* (1964) — an alien life form turns out to be a machine. Such stories are, naturally, subject to the same sorts of permutations and thematic developments as any other alien-contact narratives. Lem's point is the folly of contemplating the nonhuman world in romantic, anthropocentric terms. The deadly clouds of microscopic machines on the planet Regis are neither friends nor enemies to man. Their way of "life" has nothing to do with ours, and they and their planet should be left alone. "Not everywhere has everything been intended for us."[6]

Stories in which machines are simply instruments or simply aliens do not involve dialectical interplay between man and machine. Between these poles, however, are those fables that do concern themselves with reciprocal interaction. Many turn upon a transposition of the "natural" relationship between man and machine: man becomes the slave, the machine the master. Sometimes the story moves toward the reaffirmation of human authority as in Brian Aldiss' "But Who Can Replace a Man?" (1958), which concludes with a group of apparently independent machines meekly submitting to the first human being they encounter. And sometimes the machine is revealed as finally and absolutely the master as in Harlan Ellison's "I Have No Mouth and I Must Scream" (1967), in which a mad computer endlessly torments the last human beings alive. Logically, the master-slave relationship reaches its most extreme form in the relationship between god and man, and science fiction abounds in stories that portray machines as divinities, either

153

malevolent like Ellison's magically endowed computer – named AM – or mysteriously benevolent like the
slabs in *2001*. In Fredric Brown's "Answer" (1954) the
ultimate computer is switched on and asked whether
there is a God. "Yes, *now* there is a God," the machine
replies.[7]

More interesting than these fables, however, are
those that focus on the movement of man and
machine toward a common center. *2001* is consistently
uneasy about this movement – indeed, the film does
not conclude until it has succeeded in separating again
the ideas of the organic and the mechanical in the
complementary figures of the starchild and the slab –
and in its uneasiness it represents the dominant attitude of recent science fiction. Valuing feeling or
imagination above reason, such writers as Kurt Von-
negut or Philip K. Dick naturally regard machines with
distrust. The writers of Campbell's Golden Age,
however, committed as they were to a rationalist
ideology, were more likely to treat the subject in a
positive fashion. From this point of view, the more
perfectly man learns to control his atavistic emotion-
alism and superstitiousness – and thus the more nearly
he comes to approach the status of a rational engine –
the more fully human he becomes. Not only does the
mechanization of man pose no threat, but those who
would deny human status to worthy machines seem
benighted or illiberal.

Robert A. Heinlein's rationalistic *The Moon Is a
Harsh Mistress* (1966), for example, contrasts nicely
with *2001*. Adaptability to new circumstances is the
book's central value. The main figure here is Mike, a

sentient computer, and the novel divides its characters into "stupid" and "not stupid" according to whether they have the mental flexibility to recognize that Mike is more than a machine. Mike's "coming awake" at the novel's start illustrates the possibility of crossing mental boundaries and prefigures the political awakening of the lunar colony that has hitherto been subject to earth. Interestingly, the colonial revolutionaries' cell system is a version of a cybernetic system. Interestingly, too, the chief human character, Manny, is a kind of cyborg, possessing a set of interchangeable mechanical arms. Moreover, the landscape fuses the usually opposed conceptions of the pastoral and the industrial, the natural and the artificial. Heinlein's lunar colonists are farmers, simple and independent rustics in the true pastoral tradition. But their farming is hydroponic and their lives are lived underground in an artificial environment of tunnels and warrens. Again and again, the novel questions the validity of making a sharp distinction between the organic and the mechanical. But instead of regarding the interpenetration of man and machine with suspicion, Heinlein celebrates it as the key to a new freedom.

Like Kubrick's and Clarke's HAL, Ellison's AM, and Heinlein's Mike, machines in science fiction are continually "coming awake" and developing consciousness. Indeed, as *Frankenstein*, the archetype of the machine story, suggests, the drama of machines may ultimately be understood as a drama of consciousness. Just as nature in science fiction might be said to aspire to become animate and assume the form of the alien, so science-fiction machines aspire to become human beings. Combine artificial intelligence, sensory equipment, mobility, and the capacity to interact physically with the world and you have a robot. Whether the robot is metallic or organic in substance — in the latter case robots are sometimes called androids — is of secondary importance. What is crucial is the idea of an artificial creature that imitates a man. Situated precisely on the boundary between man and machine, robots occupy a magical position, and it is because of this that they figure so prominently in science fiction.

From Karel Capek's *R.U.R.* (1921) on, one of the characteristic concerns of robot stories has been the idea of robots replacing men. Sometimes the robot is treated negatively as a threat to humane values as in Harlan Ellison's and Ben Bova's "Brillo" (1970) in which an irritatingly literal robot is employed in police work, and sometimes the robot is treated sympathetically as it usually is in Isaac Asimov's robot stories. One of the literary games of popular science fiction has been the employment of robots in all possible human professions. Thus we have had robot nurses, doctors, lawyers, boxers, dancers, actors, and politicians. In Robert Silverberg's "Good News from the Vatican" (1971) a robot is elected pope.

More penetrating than these, however, are stories that focus directly on the fundamental question that the robot's borderline position raises: What does it mean to be human? In Philip K. Dick's satirical *Do Androids Dream of Electric Sheep?* (1968) the distinction between human beings and their coldly selfish artificial counterparts is primarily one of feeling, or "empathic capacity." Thus it requires complex psychological testing to determine whether an individual is a man or a machine. Moreover, some androids sincerely believe that they are human. The story concerns "bounty hunters," police killers who earn their living by "retiring" runaway robots. Are the bounty killers, professional murderers trained to kill in cold blood, any more human than their artificial victims?

Robot stories, like machine stories generally, tend to revolve around some form of master – slave antinomy. They also tend to incorporate some form of opposition between reason and passion, between rigidly mechanical logic and flexible human feeling. Most important, the figure of the robot, a programmed machine and yet a sentient being like ourselves, readily incorporates the central science-fiction concern with determinism and free will, and recognizing this also helps to explain its prominence in the genre.[8]

Stanislaw Lem's tale "The Mask" (1976),[9] one of the most suggestive robot fictions to date, focuses directly on the question of free will, turning a story of an artificial creature into a self-reflexive fable about literature. Just as a robot is bound by its programming, so a writer is bound by language, genre, and theme, limited by the program of a medium that is the culture's design, not his own. As Lem says in another context, "The writing of a novel is a form of the loss of creative liberty."[10] In fact, the writer's problem is that of every man, for language is thrust upon us all from the outside. The very medium of consciousness, the language in which we possess ourselves, is not our own. Even in the most intimate sphere of private thought, we too might be said to be programed.

Lem's story is a drama of consciousness. Composed

in the first person from the point of view of an anonymous robot programmed by the King to seduce and murder a courtier named Arrhodes, the narrative concerns the machine's discovery of its nature and its struggle to free itself from the instructions "written" within it. To itself as to others, the robot appears to be a beautiful lady, and at first the machine regards itself as a woman. But gradually, meditating upon certain anomalies and inconsistencies in her memories — for example, she finds that she recalls several different personal histories — she begins to suspect that her human appearance is a mask. Midway through the narrative, the woman slits her body open and exposes the silver, scorpionlike machine that is her true self. Her horrified lover flees and the story turns into a grotesque narrative of pursuit as the deadly machine tracks Arrhodes, who comes to represent the idea of free intelligence, to an isolated fortress where he dies in her arms.

Lem turns the fable back upon itself by making the robot a metaphor for his own narrative: Lem's story is also a kind of machine designed first to woo the idea of free intelligence and then to run it to death. In another sense as well, the robot is equivalent to the story, for the entire narrative, written in a run-on style that imitates thought, is finally no more than the rushing flood of words that constitutes the robot's consciousness. Repeatedly the robot draws attention to her own verbal brilliance: "I was cleverness itself, keen and full of witticisms, my eyes took on fire from the dazzling quickness of my words — in my mounting anxiety I would have gladly played a featherbrain to save Arrhodes, but this alone I could not manage. My versatility did not extend that far, alas" (pp. 193-194). Repeatedly, too, the robot speaks of her consciousness in linguistic metaphors, referring, for instance, to the moment when she discovered herself to be a woman, a "she" instead of an "it," as the moment of "the change of grammatical form" and to the disturbing fact of her multiple personal histories as "the plurality of my past pluperfects" (p. 208). Moreover, she is continually aware of herself as playing a kind of role – she has been cast in a part by the King – and she is painfully conscious of the limitations imposed upon her by the style of drama in which she is compelled to act. Meeting Arrhodes in the royal garden, she attempts to warn him to flee but finds herself unable to speak. "The style would not permit it," she confesses. "What sort of love scene is it, in which Nicolette confesses to Aucassin that she is his branding iron, his butcher?" (p. 210).

The multiple memories that play through the robot's consciousness whenever she turns inward to seek her true identity are a repertoire provided so that she will be able to assume various guises depending upon the requirements of the moment. Thus she remembers herself simultaneously as the daughter of a count, as a young duenna, and as a foreign-born orphan. This "plurality of abandoned pasts" has its equivalent in the conspicuous allusiveness of Lem's fable. Thus the opening, describing the robot's hazy recollection of its own construction, alludes simultaneously to Genesis and also perhaps to the dark and stormy nights of lightning and thunder that figure in Frankenstein films:

ALIEN ENCOUNTERS

In the beginning there was darkness and cold flame and
lingering thunder, and, in long strings of sparks, char-black
hooks, segmented hooks, which passed me on, and creeping
metal snakes that touched the thing that was me with their
snoutlike flattened heads, and each such touch brought on
a lightning tremor, sharp, almost pleasurable. (p.181)

The biblical allusion will recur in the parodic version
of the Fall that takes place in the royal garden when
the robot attempts to warn Arrhodes about herself and
thus to enlist him as an ally in her rebellion against the
King. The Frankenstein allusion also recurs — on the
chase, for instance, the robot creeps up to human
dwellings, peering through windows and listening to
conversations — and there are echoes of Hoffmann and
Kafka as well. Interestingly, when the robot first comes
to full consciousness she discovers that she is attend-
ing a court ball where she is surprised to find that the
setting is familiar and that she knows even the names
and ranks of the various assembled nobles. To us too,
"programed" as we are by our previous experience of
literature, the world of Lem's story is oddly familiar. A
king and his courtiers, a royal ball in a castle, a dimly
perceived populace of peasants, a monastery inhabited
by an honest and thoughtful monk — this is a literary
world we have visited many times before. And it is,
conspicuously, a *literary* world. In order to make its
point Lem's fable exaggerates its own literariness. But
what does literature consist of but a plurality of
abandoned pasts traversing the flow of a current
consciousness?
    Consciousness is the robot's burden, for to be con-

160

scious is inevitably to ask "Who am I?" and to this question she can find no satisfactory answer. Seeing Arrhodes for the first time, she perceives him as her alter ego and through him defines the pain that she in her utter aloneness feels. Arrhodes' face, she tells us, was "quite ordinary."

> Indeed its features had that fixed asymmetry of handsome homeliness so characteristic of intelligence, but he must have grown weary of his own bright mind, as too penetrating and also somewhat self-destructive, no doubt he ate away at himself nights, it was evident this was a burden on him, and that there were moments in which he would have been glad to rid himself of that intelligence, like a crippling thing, not a privilege or gift, for continual thought must have tormented him, particularly when he was by himself, and that for him was a frequent occurrence – everywhere, therefore here also. (p. 188)

Alone in her carriage after the ball, the robot again agonizes over her identity. The windowless dark carriage suggests her problem: Where in a complete void of information about herself can she find light? Her beautiful body and her cold intelligence both seem to her somehow alien. How can she identify her true self? She settles at last upon one certainty, Arrhodes, about whom she feels the "iron presence of destiny," an inescapable necessity that constitutes her very being. "I had been made for him, he for me" (p. 201), Lem with with characteristic irony has her say. But if necessity alone is certain, if her very being derives from something imposed upon her from outside, then what constitutes her authentic self?

In the robot's meditation, Lem is playing with a familiar philosophical conundrum, one that has been resolved in different fashions in different periods. The resolution that the robot arrives at is, we should note, the heroic posture of such romantics as Blake and Shelley: given a pervasive and all-constituting necessity, no possible authenticity exists except in rebellion and thus the genuine man must be a rebel. Vowing to rebel against the King or against herself, the robot begins to tear at the carriage's soft upholstery to expose the hard structure that it hides. Earlier the carriage's darkness suggested the void in which her intelligence found itself. Now its padded upholstery becomes an image for her new understanding of her condition, her apparently free intelligence and perfect beauty masking the iron presence of destiny within. Appropriately, considering its romantic literary antecedants, the robot's rebellion leads to her futile attempt to play Eve to Arrhodes' Adam in an inverted replay of the Fall. And, appropriately, her ultimate attempt at rebellion, the self-consciously romantic scene in which she takes the knife to herself, results not in heroic suicide but in exposing the cold, metal creature that is her true self. Even her self-evisceration, she realizes, was not free but represented "a foreseen part of the plan" (p. 215).

Shedding the mask of humanity ends the romantic agony. Language and consciousness disappear, and the machine becomes a subhuman instrument of pursuit, tracking Arrhodes across the King's lands by smell. Arrhodes, however, is too clever to be captured by a mere mechanical hound, and eventually the robot finds that she must become intelligent again. Moving toward its conclusion, the story now becomes more explicitly allegorical as the robot encounters a monk, the representative of Christian humanism, to whom she confesses that she wishes to discontinue the chase. Initially the monk refuses to regard her as capable of independent thought, but the robot's intelligent explanation of her problem and her passionate plea eventually change his opinion. The conversation with the monk is one of the few passages of dialogue in the narrative:

> "I ask you once again," he said, "tell me, what will you do when you see Arrhodes?"
> "Father, I tell you once again that I do not know, for though I wish him no evil, that which is written within me may prove more powerful than what I wish."
> Upon hearing this, he covered his eyes with his hand and said: "You are my sister." (p. 226)

From the beginning Lem's narrative has solicited the reader's identification with the robot. We have come to consciousness with it, puzzled with it over its identity, and discovered its true nature through its own thoughts. Naturally, then, the interview with the monk is cathartic, for here the story ratifies our acceptance of the machine as a creature like ourselves. Subtly, however, Lem has slipped into a more objective form of narrative, and we do not realize at first that we no longer are privy to the robot's thoughts.

Won over by the machine, the sympathetic monk reveals that Arrhodes took refuge in the monastery but that he was recently abducted by traitors to the King who wished to employ his intelligence for their own purposes. The robot spends the night in the monastery and then sets off to "free" Arrhodes. With a shock we realize that the robot is a liar, that the thoughtful conversation with the monk was only a ruse to discover Arrhodes' hiding place. The gentle monk has been deceived, and we have been deceived with him, trapped by our assumption that Lem's narrative is sincere, that the robot withholds nothing from us. But if we cannot trust the voice of the story, the voice that is in a sense our own consciousness in the narrative, then what can we trust? Lem has forced us into a position equivalent to that of the robot when it discovered that it could not trust its own mind. Hard in pursuit of Arrhodes again, the robot confesses to us directly. But no sooner does it admit its deception than it withdraws its own statement: "No doubt you would like to know what my true intentions were in that final run, and so I will tell you that I tricked the monks, and yet I did not trick them, for I truly desired to regain or rather gain my freedom, indeed I had never possessed it" (p. 231). Is the robot free or not free? What Lem has done is to tie his text into a paradox that makes a mockery of the very idea of free will. "I think therefore that I was nobly base," the machine continues, "and by freedom compelled to do not that which was commanded me directly, but that which in my incarnation I myself desired."

The landscape of the final pursuit symbolically recapitulates the story's thematic movement. Leaving the monastery, the retreat of humanism, the robot tracks Arrhodes and his abductors into a sterile wilderness. Every detail of the chase is suggestive, such as the craggy pass that is compared to "the ruin of a giant cathedral" or the high, snowy gorge that is shrouded in mist. In a mountain fortress as formidable as fate itself — "not a house, not a castle, erected with such massive stones that not even a giant could have moved one single-handed" (p. 235) — the robot at last finds Arrhodes, unconscious and dying. Tensely she waits for him to awaken, but does she mean to rescue him or kill him? Arrhodes dies without opening his eyes, the robot wraps her arms around his corpse, and together they rest in a bed of snow. Strategically ambiguous, the conclusion retreats from the abyss of speculation about the robot's nature, settling upon the obvious narrative fact that the quest is over. And thus, like the robot in the windowless carriage, the reader is left in darkness with only a single certainty to cling to, the sense of the iron presence of destiny involving the robot and the man.

In Jack Williamson's "With Folded Hands" (1947) an army of robots programed to protect people from harm takes over the world and reduces mankind to slavery. With tyrannical beneficence the robots refuse to allow men to perform any significant activity, since even the most trivial occupation might prove dangerous. As one of the robots explains, "It is no longer necessary for men to care for themselves because we exist to insure their safety and happiness."[11] Mr. Sledge, the original designer of the robots, believed he was creating a perfect world, one in which men could live free from war or other forms of self-destruction. He is appalled at the nightmare his dream has become, but all his attempts to stop the machines are futile. Distressed by Sledge's unhappiness, the robots operate on his brain, and at the end he has finally become a satisfied man, a firm believer in the goodness of the world made by the robots.

Williamson's story, describing the establishment of a totalitarian state run by machines, suggests the connection between the dystopian fables that comprise so conspicuous a part of the science-fiction canon and the story of the machine.[12] In Williamson's fable the state is literally an army of machines. In the dystopias the issue of man in conflict with machine is joined at the level of metaphor. Behind such texts as Aldous Huxley's *Brave New World* (1932), George Orwell's *Nineteen Eighty-Four* (1949), and the many antiutopian narratives of the 1950s and 1960s characteristically lies the metaphor of society as a kind of machine that has reduced the individual to the status of a robot. Thus in Frederik Pohl's and C. M. Kornbluth's caustic satire on a world dominated by advertising agencies, *The Space Merchants* (1953), men have been programed to race in circles of consumption: "Think about smoking, think about Starrs, light a Starr. Light a Starr, think about Popsie, get a squirt. Get a squirt, think about Crunchies, buy a box. Buy a box, think about smoking, light a Starr."[13] And even the advertising executives themselves have been programed to believe in the righteousness of their lives, to behave as if the highest ideal were indeed Sales. As in the case of Williamson's unstoppable robots, so the debasing social system in

Pohl's and Kornbluth's world is self-regulating and out of control.

A man who behaves like a machine is a man possessed. Dystopias are thus in a sense stories of possession and, like all such tales, they are concerned with freedom. The typical dystopian narrative involves a choice between happiness and freedom, the happiness of total surrender of the will to society or the freedom of individual choice. But surrender may also be viewed as freedom, liberation from responsibility, just as independence may be viewed as happiness. Characteristically, the dystopian plot enacts the exorcism of the daemonic spirit from the mind of the protagonist — or, to change the metaphor, the deprograming of the protagonist, who then becomes an enemy of the mechanized society. In the process, the protagonist's mental universe is turned upside down as he is compelled to redefine all the concepts through which he lives. The issue in these narratives, then, is ultimately one of opposed points of view, and thus the dystopia, like the robot story, readily becomes a drama of consciousness. This is most clear perhaps in the first, and in many ways still the best, of the major dystopias, Yevgeny Zamiatin's We (1924)[14] Indeed, We can be seen as an inversion of "The Mask." In Lem's narrative a human consciousness discovers that it is a machine. In Zamiatin's a mechanized consciousness discovers that it is a man.

The plot of We is simple. Set in the "One State," a walled city-state of the far future, the narrative centers on D-503, builder of the Integral, the spaceship through which the state intends to export "the beneficent yoke of reason" to the "unknown beings on other planets" (p. 3). In this context Zamiatin develops a classic love story in which D-503 abandons 0-90, his affectionate, childlike lover, for the mysterious I-330, who turns out to be a member of a revolutionary organization. The revolutionaries unsuccessfully attempt to seize the *Integral*, I-330 is captured, and at the end D-503, who like Williamson's Mr. Sledge has been subjected to a brain operation, calmly watches I-330 tortured to death.

The simplicity of the plot makes possible the novel's complex surface. Zamiatin presents his story through D-503 in a series of diary entries, fragments that begin and end abruptly, sometimes shift unexpectedly in midstream, and characteristically leave much unsaid. The narrative is fragmented because there is no single, integrated personality controlling it. D-503 is literally a man without a personality – or, rather, he is a schizophrenic personality, divided between his identity-less identity as a "number of the State" and his "other self," the "soul" that begins to grow within him as a consequence of his relationship with I-330. Ironically, it is the very act of writing the journal that begins the process of D-503's fragmentation. At the start, his voice and the state's are indistinguishable. Indeed, the novel opens with a word-for-word transcription of a state proclamation urging all numbers to compose poems and eulogies to be carried on board the *Integral*. Since his thoughts are identical to those of the state, D-503 explains, his journal will be a kind of poem in honor of the state's perfect life. As for himself, he says he feels "something similar to what a woman feels when she first senses within herself the pulse of a new, still tiny, still blind little human being" (p. 4).

MACHINE

Machines are dead matter, people are alive. Machine stories, including the dystopias, tend to be fairly explicit versions of the struggle between life and death, embodiments of the fear that life may become indistinguishable from death. Sexuality signifies life and thus commonly represents a threat to the dystopian state, which seeks to subvert or control vitality. In Huxley's *Brave New World,* for instance, the state has mechanized reproduction, manufacturing citizens in hatcheries, and intercourse has been trivialized through state-sponsored promiscuity. In *We,* too, sexuality is the business of the state. According to the *Lex Sexualis,* each number has a right to use any other number as a sexual commodity, but only after obtaining a license. A pink coupon is issued, and thereafter the numbers may engage in sexual relations on specified days and at specified hours. Appropriately, given the threat of sexuality to the state, Zamiatin presents the idea of individuality stirring within D-503 in a sexual metaphor. We can note, too, that D-503's figurative pregnancy is echoed later in the novel when 0-90, who is too short to meet the state's "maternal norm," becomes unlawfully pregnant, an act that represents her personal rebellion against the barrenness to which the state has condemned her. Moreover, the novel as a whole can be read as a tale of sexual awakening, the story of D-503's passion attempting to burst into flower.

Art also signifies life, and thus the dystopian state generally seeks to mechanize this form of creation as well.[15] Significantly, one of the background figures in *We* is a professional poet, R-13, whose unsatisfactory role in the state is the versification of such official

169

documents as the Death Sentence. As D-503 proudly explains, "Our poets no longer soar in the empyrean; they have come down to earth; they stride beside us to the stern mechanical March of the Music Plant" (p. 61). For D-503, as for the One State, beauty means clarity, regularity, and mechanical repetition. Watching a gang of laborers bending and unbending "like the levers of a single huge machine," D-503 is struck by the poetry of the sight: "It was the highest, the most stirring beauty, harmony, music" (p. 74). Comically, Zamiatin has D-503 refer to The Railroad Guide as the "greatest literary monument to have come down to us from ancient days" (p. 12). But, even in the most unpromising soil, art will attempt to flower, and, ironically, D-503 discovers that his own work is nothing like what he originally intended, that "instead of a harmonious and strict mathematical poem in honor of the One State" his journal has become "a fantastic adventure novel" (p. 91).

Fully committed to the world view of the state, D-503 embraces the conception of himself as a machine. He speaks happily about his brain as a "gleaming mechanism" and boasts about the way the Table of Hours governs the numbers' lives:

Why, it transforms each one of us into a figure of steel, six-wheeled hero of a mighty epic poem. Every morning, with six-wheeled precision, at the same hour and the same moment, we — millions of us — get up as one. At the same hour, in million-headed unison, we start work; and in million-headed unison we end it.   (pp.12–13)

MACHINE

Ironically, he conceives his passion in terms of mathematics, identifying I-330 and the nameless feelings she releases in him with the dreaded "irrational root," the square root of minus one. D-503's passions appear to him to belong to a completely alien creature, one he associates with his hairy hands, and the struggle between his two selves becomes a nightmarish agony. It is not a situation he can long endure, for, as he explains, he is like a motor that is being run too fast and soon will melt from overheating.

But in fact there is no life for D-503, except in continuing struggle. On the one hand is the form of death represented by the state, which acknowledges only the claims of reason, and on the other is a passion that is finally no less a form of death. Total commitment either to reason or to passion leads to the dissolution of the self. From the first, the image of I-330 with her disturbingly sharp white teeth hints at the predator, and, as we discover, her purposes in seducing D-503 are indeed predatory. Like the state, she too is a kind of daemon, a succubus who seeks to turn D-503 into her slave so that through him the revolutionaries can gain control of the *Integral*. Perversely, D-503 is drawn to I-330 rather than to the genuinely loving 0-90 precisely because of the woman's will to dominate him. Sensing that his passion involves death, that, as he in a characteristic mathematical metaphor puts it, love is the "function" of death, D-503 acknowledges his fear of I-330. "That's the horror of it, that even today, when the logical function has been integrated, when it is obvious that death is implicit in this function, I still

171

desire her, with my lips, arms, breast, with every millimeter of me" (p. 119). D-503's real desire is simply to lose himself in the will of another, either that of the state or that of the woman. Unable to bear the heat of the continual struggle that the novel identifies as life, he is ultimately in love with death.

Appropriately, D-503's final wish is to commit suicide. "It is the same as killing myself — but perhaps this is the only way to resurrection" (p. 197), he says, explaining his decision to confess his involvement with the revolutionaries to the police. Ironically, the policeman to whom he speaks turns out to be a revolutionary. Nevertheless, the state soon helps to fulfill his desire. A brain operation, a surgical method for the removal of the "imagination," has been devised to pacify the citizens. "REJOICE! For henceforth you shall be perfect!" announces the proclamation urging all numbers to submit to the procedure. "Until this day, your own creations — machines — were more perfect than you," it continues, explaining that the major difference between citizens and machines is that machines have no imagination, and that now the path to machinelike perfection is open (p. 153). Operated upon and happy at last, D-503 attains the relief from the burden of living that he has all along sought.

The ultimate machine in *We,* the central image of the novel, is the city itself, the sterile world constructed out of glass as flawless and transparent as reason.[16] The One State was created, we learn, after a two-hundred-year war between the city and the country that concluded with the building of the Green Wall.

MACHINE

Oh, great, divinely bounding wisdom of walls and barriers! They are, perhaps, the greatest of man's inventions. Man ceased to be a wild animal only when he built the first wall. Man ceased to be a savage only when we had built the Green Wall, when we had isolated our perfect mechanical world from the irrational, hideous world of trees, birds, animals. (p. 83)

Inside the wall is the realm of death; outside is the vital realm of nature, a riot of color and spontaneous movement that D-503 finds alarming. Appropriately, the revolutionaries gather beyond the wall, gaining access to the countryside through the Ancient House, a boundary locale that is neither wholly of the city nor wholly of the land. It is here that D-503 and I-330 generally meet, and D-503 refers to this place, the point at which life and death intersect, as the "starting point of all the coordinates in this entire story" (p. 82).

From one point of view I-330 may be a succubus, but in the larger context of the novel suggested by the city and the countryside she, like the revolutionary party, is the agent of life. The revolutionaries call themselves Mephi — from "Mephisto" — a name that both suggests the diabolic and also identifies them as opponents of any neo-Christian notion of final perfection such as that embodied in the secular New Jerusalem of the glass city. "There are two forces in the world — entropy and energy," I-330 says. "One leads to blissful quietude, to happy equilibrium; the other, to destruction of equilibrium, to tormentingly endless movement" (p. 144). Committed to energy, to the continual struggle that is life, the Mephi's goal is the de-

173

struction of the city wall, the breaking down of all walls "to let the green wind blow free from end to end – across the earth" (p. 137).

The artificial versus the natural, city versus country, logic versus love, death versus life – by the end of the novel all these concerns have been reinterpreted so that they may also be understood in terms of closure versus openness. Behind the utopian striving lies an act of denial that has its source in the fear of the infinite. Thus the closed, protecting city – ironically, the *Integral's* purpose is really only the extension of the city walls – and thus, too, the state's claim to have ended the need for further struggle. As I-330 explains, the founders of the state came to suppose that theirs was the ultimate revolution, that they were the "final number." But since the number of numbers is infinite, how can there be a final number? "Children are frightened by infinity," I-330 says, "and it's important that children sleep peacefully at night" (p. 152). We should note that the denial of tomorrow involves the denial of free will. If the present is an eternity, perfect and unchanging, then the idea of free will becomes meaningless, as indeed it does from the state's point of view. From the novel's point of view, however, the utopians have become robots. The desire for perfection is the desire for death.

Committed to openness, the novel ends in irresolution. I-330 is captured and executed. Significantly, she is murdered in the Bell, a great glass jar reminiscent of the enclosed city from which the air is evacuated until she strangles. Nevertheless, 0-90, illegally pregnant and thus condemned to death, has escaped beyond the walls. Moreover, the walls themselves have been breached, birds are in the air, leaves are scattered on the streets. There is fighting in the city, but whether the state or the revolutionaries will triumph is uncertain. Ironically, D-503, lobotomized and calm, is in no doubt about the outcome: "I am certain we shall conquer. Because Reason must prevail." At the end as at the beginning, his voice is indistinguishable from the state's.

MONSTER

Disemboweling herself, Stanislaw Lem's narrator in "The Mask" exposes a glittering, deadly machine, a monster of relentless logic. "The Mask" is, we might say, a fable of self-alienation. Separated from physical nature, disconnected from his own creations, modern man characteristically distrusts himself as well, and this form of alienation also plays a significant role in science fiction.

The concept of self-alienation is recent, deriving from Hegel, but the phenomenon – the feeling of estrangement from the self – cannot be located historically in the same manner as, say, the sense of alienation from nature. Indeed, there is some question about whether self-alienation is a historical phenomenon at all or whether it is an essential property of consciousness. Here, however, we need only observe that in one form or another self-alienation has been a prominent theme in Western thought at least since the early Renaissance when Protestant theology began to place such an enormous emphasis on the individual consciousness and on the old Adam lurking within. In various ways self-alienation figures in Marxist, Freudian, and Existentialist thought, and we also of course find it as a recurring theme in such central writers in the English tradition as Wordsworth and Matthew Arnold. In poetry it often takes the form of an elegiac lament for a lost wholeness, as in Arnold's "The Buried Life" with its melancholy sense of separation from the "hidden self," the true self toward which we never seem able to be faithful.[1]

Many science-fiction narratives involve the dis-

176

MONSTER

covery of a buried life, a hidden self. In the movie *Forbidden Planet* (1956), a spaceship crew investigating an alien world is threatened by a monster. Once the home of a technologically advanced race, the Krel, the planet is now inhabited by the two survivors of an earlier exploratory mission, Dr. Morbius, who has devoted himself to studying the Krel, and his daughter. Apparently the epitome of cold intellect, the scientific reason embodied, Dr. Morbius is in fact a man of intense passions that he has never acknowledged. The creature that attacks the crew turns out to be Morbius' own savage unconsciousness – "Monsters from the id!" one of the characters exclaims – amplified and materialized by Krel technology. Dr. Morbius and his daughter live in an elegant, sleekly rational house set amongst carefully designed gardens. But a secret passage in the study opens to the underworld of the Krel machines, a vast subterranean realm of enormous power that suggests the hidden landscape of Dr. Morbius' mind. The film's message is clear. Beneath man's rational surface lurks a demon. Multiply man's power through technology and the power of unreason is also multiplied.

Forbidden Planet is a version of *The Tempest* with Dr. Morbius' monster in the role of Caliban, the "thing of darkness" that Prospero finally acknowledges as his own. Caliban represents, among other things, the unregenerate, earthy side of man – original sin, we should say if we were to read the play as a Christian allegory – that must be restrained in order to found a civil society. Drawing upon the popular mythology of Freudian psychology, the id-monster of *Forbidden*

177

Planet represents something analogous, and the possibility of translating Caliban into such a figure indicates the continuity between certain older forms of self-alienation and our own.

"The Mask" and *Forbidden Planet* taken together suggest the terms in which self-distrust typically manifests itself. On the one hand is the dread of being taken over by the machine of pure logic, a form of anxiety that a Freudian might identify as the fear of the superego. As in *We,* this anxiety often expresses itself as a fear of the future, an uncertainty about what we may become. On the other is the dread of the wild man within, the fear of a savage passion that might burst out to devour everything we value.[2] As in *The Drowned World,* where this anxiety finds expression in a peculiarly passive form, the fear of the wild man often manifests itself as an anxiety about what we may have been, a dread of the return of an older, archaic self. In all fables of self-alienation the issue can be understood as one of authenticity. Which is the authentic creature in "The Mask," the consciousness that feels itself to be free or the programed machine? Which is the authentic man in *Forbidden Planet,* the rational scientist or the raging monster?

Alternatively, the sense of the buried self may express itself in a positive form as a hope that the hidden creature will be superior to the manifest self. Thus we have the many stories of magical powers supposed to be buried deep within the mind. A. E. Van Vogt's *Slan* (1940), the story of a telepathic boy who, like others of his mutant race, is hated and feared by normal men, is a well-known narrative of this sort. Such

powers as telepathy, precognition, telekinesis, and
teleportation are generally imagined as appearing first
among children and frequently among social outcasts.
According to the romantic ideology that controls most
stories of hidden mental powers, children and outcasts,
being less fully socialized than others, have greater access to their unconscious selves. The distinction between superiority and monstrosity is of course simply a
matter of point of view. Van Vogt's novel asks us to
regard Jommy Cross as a superior creature, but to the
rest of mankind he is a monster. Thus stories of secret
mental powers readily collapse back from fables of
desire into fables of fear, as in Jerome Bixby's "It's a
Good Life" (1953) in which a child tyrannically rules a
small community with his dreadful psychic powers.

In science fiction, feelings of self-alienation typically express themselves as narratives of metamorphosis, stories of the transformation of man into
something less than or more than human. Dehuman-
ized man, man as either monster or superman, is in
principle indistinguishable from any other kind of
alien, and the figures in such stories are sometimes
synonymous with aliens. In Larry Niven's *Protector*
(1973) mankind turns out to be the undeveloped form
of an alien species, the Pak. Millions of years ago the
Pak seeded the earth with their own kind, but, lacking
a particular enzyme that develops only in a special
form of Pak food, the human race has remained in the
"breeder stage," never reaching the full adult phase of
the species. Though vastly more intelligent than man,
the Pak are not simply our superiors. In fact, they are
monsters both of reason and of passion. Repeatedly

we hear that for the Pak there are almost no choices in life; like computing machines, they always see the single best solution to any problem in a flash and then are bound to follow the course that logic dictates. At the same time, however, they are creatures of brutish instinct whose single concern is the protection of their progeny. Forever at war with one another, the Pak represent not a hope but a threat to fundamental human values.

The story of transformation is the correlative of the story of alien confrontation. Instead of meeting the alien across a barrier of otherness, man discovers himself to be in some sense the alien. Thus the feeling of self-estrangement, as expressed in science fiction, may be understood as the correlative of the feeling of alienation from the external universe. And thus, too, the feeling of self-estrangement may be regarded as the element that completes the underlying structure of science fiction, complementing and balancing all the externalized forms of the genre's concern.

The confrontation with the nonhuman generally involves some form of transformation. We recall that in H. G. Wells's "The Star" the near collision with the stray planet changes the earth, releasing floods, earthquakes, and volcanic eruptions. Nor do matters return to normal after the holocaust. The moon is smaller, the sun larger, and the earth's climate hotter so that the centers of human life must shift northward and southward toward the poles. Moreover, the mention of a new brotherhood among men suggests that humanity has been affected in other ways as well.

MONSTER

In *The War of the Worlds* the earth is at least temporarily changed, and here again the physical change is associated with a psychic change in humanity. The narrator emerges from captivity in the ruined house to a strange world of Martian vegetation. "I found about me the landscape, weird and lurid, of another planet," he says, and then describes the great scarlet and crimson plants that line the way to Kew as "an avenue of gigantic blood-drops" (p. 424). The blood-red Martian growth suggests the alien ruthlessness that is contrasted from the start of the novel with human sympathy and kindness. But the text casts doubt upon the appropriateness of any absolute dichotomy between the human and the Martian, reminding us — as in its evocation of the European slaughter of the Tasmanians — that we too possess the potential for inhuman ruthlessness. The artilleryman dreams of seizing one of the Martian machines:

Just imagine this: Four or five of their fighting-machines suddenly starting off — Heat-Rays right and left, and not a Martian in 'em. Not a Martian in 'em, but men — men who have learned the way how. It may be in my time, even — those men. Fancy having one of them lovely things, with its Heat-Ray wide and free!   (pp. 435–436)

The triumph that the artilleryman envisions is, in effect, to become a Martian.[3]

Even in *Journey to the Centre of the Earth* the potential for transformation is hinted when Axel and his uncle encounter the prehistoric giant. Sometimes the idea of transformation is peripheral. Sometimes,

181

too, as in *The War of the Worlds,* the narrative stops
short of portraying an actual metamorphosis. The
transformation may be treated negatively as the appearance of monstrosity, or it may be treated positively as a fulfillment of human nature, as in
Bowman's metamorphosis at the end of *2001.* Always,
however, the confrontation with the nonhuman is at
least potentially a dynamic, reciprocal affair.

As in Niven's *Protector,* it is sometimes a cosmic influence, a visitor from space, that transforms man into
the alien. Probably the best-known of such stories is
Arthur C. Clarke's *Childhood's End* (1953) in which a
benevolent alien race, the Overlords, saves mankind
from self-destruction and for a time establishes a
utopia. The Overlords' true purpose, however, is to ad-
minister the transformation of mankind into a race
able to join the Overmind, a transcendent cosmic consciousness. With the proper conditions established by
the Overlords, who are themselves totally lacking in
the latent psychic powers of mankind and thus forever
excluded from the Overmind, a spontaneous metamorphosis spreads like a disease among the world's
children. The telepathically fused entity that the
children become is horrifying precisely because it is in
superficial appearance still human. But, as the novel
insists, the children are no longer to be thought of in
human terms, having become something much greater
than either men or Overlords. Their duty as attendants
completed, the Overlords depart, and the narrative
concludes with the last man alive reporting the final
transfiguration of the children as the Earth is con-
sumed and the inhuman creature that mankind has

become leaves matter itself behind and ascends to the stars.

In *Childhood's End,* the Overmind provides the conditions that enable the metamorphosis to occur. Often, however, time is the factor that transfigures man, either brutalizing him as in the case of the Eloi and the Morlocks in *The Time Machine* or elevating him, as in the case of the races of the far future in *Last and First Men.* An entire subcategory of science fiction deals with the appearance of the superman, the next stage in human evolution. Olaf Stapledon's *Odd John* (1935), in which the telepathic supermen eventually commit suicide in a display of superior spiritual consciousness, is perhaps the richest of these stories. Probably the best-known among the more recent superman fables, however, is Theodore Sturgeon's *More Than Human* (1953), in which young outcasts possessing supernormal mental powers join together to form a new kind of collaborative telepathic entity, Homo Gestalt. Sturgeon's interesting but somewhat sentimental narrative describes the formation of the group, its maturation, and ultimately its discovery of the existence of many other gestalt beings throughout history.

Finally, as in the dystopian fables, man himself, either directly or through machines, may be the agent for his transformation. In Harlan Ellison's "I Have No Mouth, and I Must Scream," the mad computer's last act of revenge against humanity is to alter its one remaining prisoner, turning him into a shapeless monster unable either to protest or to commit suicide. Science fiction abounds in postatomic war narratives in which mutants such as those that figure in the background of

Miller's *A Canticle for Leibowitz* live monstrous half-lives, often excluded from "true men." There are also, of course, innumerable stories of genetic engineering and of cyborgs, creatures part-human and part-machine such as the man-monster designed to live on Mars in Frederik Pohl's *Man Plus* (1976). Interestingly, the engineered deformation of man is often presented as a requirement of the conquest of space. In Cordwainer Smith's fine "Scanners Live in Vain" (1948), a guild of surgically altered men runs the ships that carry ordinary people in hibernation cylinders from world to world. Only Scanners, their brains severed from all their senses except their eyes so that they can bear the "Great Pain of Space," can know the beauty of the stars: the price of knowledge is monstrosity. And in Poul Anderson's "Call Me Joe" (1957), a cripple who is telepathically linked to an artificial organism designed to live on Jupiter chooses to transfer his consciousness permanently to the puppet creature and thus becomes a Jovian. In such fables science fiction incorporates its sense not merely of the molding of the nonhuman to human purposes but also of the consequent transformations of man that are implicit in his dialogue with the universe.

Since the universe is limitless, so too are the possible shapes of man; here again we find the pervasive science-fiction concern with infinity. The vision of the genre as a whole is the conviction of infinite human plasticity. Man in science fiction is immersed in change; he may become a Martian or a Jovian, a machine or a god, a roaring monster or a telepathic superman, but always he is in the process of transformation. As in *2001,* any appearance of calm, stability, permanence, is an illusion. *Last and First Men* with its vision of continual metamorphosis as mankind works out its destiny in relation to time and to physical nature may be taken as the epitome of the genre. Of course any point of view can be inverted. In *Solaris* Lem dramatizes the rigidity of human thought in the face of the plastic universe represented by the ever-changing planet. But though the perspective is altered, the issues remain the same, cast now in the inter-rogative rather than the declarative mode. Is man plastic enough to negotiate with the cosmos?

Perhaps now the Renaissance should be invoked one last time in connection with that period's well-known concern with man's Protean qualities. The Renaissance sense of human plasticity – in Pico della Mirandola's *Oratio de hominis dignitate* and elsewhere, Proteus is a common figure for man – does indeed mark a departure from the medieval sense of man's fixed position in the order of things. Thus we have the new prominence in the sixteenth and seventeenth centuries of the old metaphor of the world as a stage on which a man may act various roles. And yet, though men might seek to change roles, they did not generally assume that the play itself was of their own making. Man might aspire to become a little lower than the angels, or might find himself reduced to a position a little above the beasts, but all his Protean changes of shape still took place within the abiding frame of what is often called the Elizabethan world picture. Later, of course, the frame itself became unstable, and, later still, it became apparent that the frame through which we perceive the world is indeed a frame, something at least in part our own creation. The modern universe is not only far vaster than that of Pico's time but also in every way more fluid and uncertain. Nevertheless, the Protean vision of science fiction clearly has roots in the Renaisssance and its new conviction of human possibility.[4]

The grotesque, as Wolfgang Kayser suggests, may be understood as an aesthetic form associated with the violation of conceptual categories such as vegetable and animal, animal and human, dead and living. Such images as plants that culminate in animal torsos, men with the heads of beasts, or corpses that dance and sing draw their power from the boundaries they transgress, implying the dissolution of the laws that govern the familiar world. The grotesque is the estranged world, the world made over according to new principles. It involves the invocation of the dark forces that lurk behind our world, threatening its disintegration. Through their portrayal in art the ominous powers are discovered and challenged. Thus the grotesque can be understood as "an attempt to invoke and subdue the demonic aspects of the world."[5]

As a literature of estrangement, concerned both with human and with world transformations, science fiction inevitably tends to the grotesque, tends to produce such images as the androgynous Gethenians of *The Left Hand of Darkness,* the two-headed Mrs. Grales of *A Canticle for Leibowitz,* or the monstrous children of *Childhood's End.* HAL's prolonged death in *2001* is grotesque, as are the swifter, mechanical deaths of the

hibernating astronauts in the Jupiter ship. We encounter the grotesque everywhere in science fiction,
from Verne's underground world complete with
mastadons and primitive man to Heinlein's lunar
pastoral or Dick's orientalized San Francisco. Indeed,
the grotesque may be considered the characteristic
aesthetic form of the genre.

The grotesque implies the daemonic.[6] I have
already noted that dystopias may be interpreted as
stories of possession. In fact, most fictions of metamorphosis may be read as fables of the daemonic,
whether the powers released are maleficent as in *Forbidden Planet* or beneficent as in *Slan*. We also commonly find the daemonic located in those figures conceived as agents of the universe: Wells's Martians and
his Morlocks, the embodiments respectively of space
and time; Lem's Phi-creatures; Stapledon's mysterious
narrator of the far future; Clarke's Overlords; or
Niven's Pak. In *The Man in the High Castle,* Hawthorne
Abendsen explicitly calls Juliana Frink, who mediates
between Dick's world and our own, a "daemon," a "little chthonic spirit" (p. 251). In *2001* HAL, who mediates
between the organic and the inorganic and between
man and the infinity of space, is kind of ghost able to
manifest himself in any part of the vessel he haunts.
All mediating figures, whether machines of human
origin or monsters or supermen of evolutionary or extraterrestrial origin, move readily toward the daemonic,
playing roles in science fiction analogous to those of
the good or evil spirits of older forms of romance. The
ultimate daemonic power is the infinite itself, the
science-fiction equivalent of god, and the tendency of

science fiction to move toward the daemonic is evidently related to the problem of the representation of the infinite. In dealing with formlessness, literature falls back upon an inherited vocabulary of archaic forms.

The activity of science fiction is a continuing play with the categories of the familiar and the unfamiliar, the human and the nonhuman, and it is through this play that the grotesque is generated. The transformed human is equivalent to the alien. Likewise, the alien may be redefined as human, a process that also results in the production of the grotesque. We can note now that, as a general rule, all science-fiction narratives can be interpreted in terms of redefinitions, reconceptions of the boundary between the human and the nonhuman. In Sturgeon's *More Than Human*, for example, Homo Gestalt is at first treated as something alien. But at the end, when the novel reveals the existence of other gestalt groups throughout history, the collaborative creature is redefined as something that has always been an integral part of humanity.

In a sense, the activity of science fiction is a process of naming. Sometimes this activity is implicit as in *More Than Human* and sometimes it is explicit as in *Journey to the Centre of the Earth*. We recall Lidenbrock and Axel's concern with finding the appropriate name for each stratum or species and also their imposition of such names as Axel Island and Cape Saknussemm upon the features of the underground world. To name the nameless is to subdue the void to human meaning, to give shape to chaos. Alternatively, texts may enact a process of renaming. The action of Cord-

MONSTER

wainer Smith's "The Game of Rat and Dragon" (1955), which describes men and cats collaborating telepathically in a struggle against giant malevolent creatures that inhabit the void of interstellar space, may be taken to be the renaming of cats, their transfer from the category nonhuman to the category human. The formless monsters of the deep in this story have two names and thus ultimately no "real" name at all; the cats perceive them as huge rats, the men as huge dragons. The cats, on the other hand, have such individuated and memorable names as Captain Wow, Lady May, and Murr. Smith's mysterious monsters, the rats and dragons of the title, imply the problematics of naming, and other texts develop such problematics into an explicit theme. *Solaris* may be read as a search for language, a quest for names to apply to the nameless.[7] What names can adequately describe the phenomena of the ocean? "Phi-creatures," "polytheria," "succubi," "phantoms" – significantly, the visitors are called by many different names. As Kris Kelvin remarks in connection with Giese's manifestly inadequate system of terminology for Solarian phenomena, "no semantic system is as yet available to illustrate the behavior of the ocean" (p. 120).

The activity of science fiction is ongoing and expansive: the conquest of any one version of the alien, the demystification of the future or of the far away, inevitably opens further vistas of mystery, deeper in time or deeper in space.[8] Clarke's "The Sentinel" (1951), the story from which *2001* was developed, presents the moon as having become an essentially human realm, one that may be explored at leisure and in relative comfort. The story concerns the rediscovery of the excitement of the alien in the form of a strange pyramid, clearly the artifact of a civilization more advanced than our own, which the lunar explorers find on a remote mountaintop. The narrative redefines the status of man. At the start, humanity is presented as a mature race, one even somewhat jaded by the wide range of its experience. At the end, contrasted with the much wider experience of the unknown race that millions of years earlier installed the pyramid on the moon, man is redefined as an infant, a race barely out of its cradle. Clarke's narrator speculates about the alien machine's purpose, suggesting that perhaps it is a kind of fire alarm, a warning system designed to tell its makers that it has been discovered by an intelligent race. But what of the aliens themselves? What are their purposes? "Perhaps they wish to help our infant civilization. But they must be very, very old, and the old are often insanely jealous of the young."[9] The story ends in mystery and uncertainty.

In Clarke's story, the renaming of the moon, its transfer from the category of the exotic to the domestic, leads to the reappearance of the nonhuman as the still more exotic alien race signified by the pyramid. Likewise, the transfer of the cats from the category of the nonhuman to the human in "The Game of Rat and Dragon" involves the appearance of the alien in the form of the nameless monsters of the void. These narratives move out toward the magical far reaches of space to discover the daemonic, but the movement may equally well be toward the magical center of the earth or of man, as in *Journey to the Centre of the*

Earth or *The Drowned World*. No matter in which direction the narrative moves, however, the process is the same. Beyond the point where the landscape is clearly defined, the alien, nameless and inchoate, is always reappearing, represented by a sign such as the pyramid or the conspicuously inadequate term "dragon" that necessarily distances the thing signified still further. And the thing itself, charged with the mystery of unthinkable otherness, is always identifiable as a version of the infinite. Science fiction, we might say, is the attempt to name the infinite.

Earlier I specified the content of science fiction as a displacement of religion. Now that content may be further specified as the sense of the infinite or, rather, as the sense of the finitude of the self, the conscious ego, in relation to the boundlessness of the cosmos that is not the self. This is indeed a religious theme, possibly the paramount religious theme. But it is also a central theme of modern psychology. Whether we follow Freud or Piaget, the main line of thought is the same: only gradually do we come in childhood to construct a world based upon the distinction between the self and the other. Moreover, as we also know, the line between the self and the other is never drawn permanently, set down in adament once and for all. Just as the child is forever involved in distinguishing himself from the parent, so the parent is forever involved in distinguishing himself from the child, both the child of his body and the child of his former self. The distinction between the self and the other is dynamic, breaking down and being reconstructed as long as life lasts.

The idea of the "nonhuman" is the idea of the "other"
writ large. Seen in this light, the content of science
fiction can be understood as a version of the fundamental dichotomy through which we conceive our
existence.

The psychological theme is evident in, say, Heinlein's "All You Zombies," where only the narcissistic,
self-created "I" remains as real, or in Ray Bradbury's
"The Martian" (1950), in which a telepathic alien
repeatedly changes its identity in response to human
emotional needs. Overwhelmed by irreconcilable de-
mands, and thus unable to maintain any single identity, the Martian flashes from shape to shape until, ex-
hausted at last, it melts into formlessness and dies. In
James Blish's "Common Time" (1953), a kind of science-
fiction version of a medieval dream vision, an astronaut traveling faster than light experiences strange
temporal effects that totally isolate him from his environment. The traveler's sense of identity disinte-
grates, but, having lost the sense of the self, he is able
to communicate directly with the angelic "beademun-
gen," natives of another star system. When he returns
to earth, the traveler's normal identity also returns;
however, he is now unable to communicate the content of his experience.

Understanding the relationship of the psychological
dichotomy to the science-fiction opposition between
the human and the nonhuman helps to explain the
manner in which such narratives as *Journey to the Centre of the Earth*, *The War of the Worlds*, or *The Time
Machine* — stories that at a literal level are almost
exclusively concerned with events in the external

world – acquire resonance and an aura of psychological significance. Reinterpreting science fiction in this
way also helps to explain the genre's interest in such
far-fetched tales as Robert Sheckley's *Mindswap* (1966),
in which the protagonist changes bodies with an alien,
or Philip K. Dick's amusing "Beyond Lies the Wub"
(1952), in which a man who eats an alien turns into the
alien. In Sheckley's story the protagonist's human consciousness persists while his body changes; in Dick's
the human body persists while the consciousness
changes. In both, however, the focus of the narrative – like the focus of so many other science-fiction
narratives – is the magical permeability of the boundary between the self and the other.

Often, as in the film *The Invasion of the Body
Snatchers*, science fiction expresses the fear of the dissolution of the self. At least as often, however, science
fiction expresses the desire to escape the prisonhouse
of the self, the wish to merge with the other, and it is
in connection with this impulse that telepathy characteristically figures. Sturgeon's *More Than Human*,
which dwells at length upon the loneliness of the outcasts before they merge to form Homo Gestalt, is an
explicit treatment of this desire. Le Guin's *The Left
Hand of Darkness* is a richer and more sophisticated
treatment of the same impulse. Appropriately, Genly
Ai's achievement of mutual understanding with the
alien Estraven is ratified by the accomplishment at last
of "mindspeaking," direct telepathic communication.

Again and again, science-fiction stories move toward apocalyptic visions of the ultimate dissolution of
the self. In *Journey to the Centre of the Earth*, Axel

dreams of dissolving in the void of space, his body
mingling like an atom with the "vast vapours tracing
their flaming orbits through infinity." In *Last and First
Men*, the eighteenth men are able to achieve an ecstatic condition in which the entire race merges into a
single entity that "sees with all eyes, and comprehends
in a single vision all visual fields" and thus "perceives
at once and as a continuous, variegated sphere, the
whole surface of the planet." In *We*, D-503 at last
achieves dissolution by melting completely into the
voice of the state. In *Childhood's End*, the transformed
children are absorbed in a column of fire into the
Overmind. "Contact," the Solarists' goal, would be another such apocalypse, as would the attaining of the
ultimate southerly point in *The Drowned World*.

Sometimes the apocalypse is presented as a vision
of death, as in *We* or in *The Time Machine* where the
traveler stands at the far verge of the earth's history
and feels the horror of the darkness and the cold. In
such cases, as in Zamiatin and Wells and also in
Zoline's "The Heat Death of the Universe," the idea of
entropy is frequently invoked and the controlling image is of the return to universal chaos and night. Alternatively, the apocalypse may be a vision of the attainment of true life, as at the end of *2001*. Finally,
however, at the far point of apocalypse the distinction
between life and death, the desirable and the horrible,
collapses. To merge with the infinite is to become
everything and nothing at once.

Many of the apocalyptic visions of science fiction
invoke the infantile or the archaic, the time before
adulthood as in the image of the transcendent child of

2001 or the time before the appearance of humanity as in *The Time Machine* or *The Drowned World*. These visions serve as clues to the nature of the nostalgia that the genre often expresses, the longing for the time before the birth into consciousness, before the knowledge of good and evil and the exile into the world.[10] Because it lies beyond consciousness, beyond language, the apocalyptic moment is unrealizable in narrative. And yet, because it represents the logical limit of the dialectic between the human and the nonhuman, science fiction inevitably moves toward apocalypse. Meaningless in itself, the idea of apocalypse is nevertheless the necessary condition for the creation of meaning through the genre. At that far point, the separation between self and other, human and nonhuman, collapses, as does any distinction between past and future, finite and infinite, matter and spirit, necessity and freedom. All the terms that constitute the substance of science fiction disappear. Alienation ends, and the empty universe becomes once more replete with significance.

NOTES

1 GENRE

1. "Science Fiction: Its Nature, Faults and Virtues," in *The Science Fiction Novel*, ed. Basil Davenport (Chicago: Advent, 1959), p. 22. One factor often at play in definitions of science fiction is rhetorical rather than analytic. Discussions of science fiction typically operate on the assumption that the genre is in need of defense against a hostile audience, and in this sort of campaign a carefully designed definition can be useful. Kingsley Amis is much more subtle than Heinlein, and his well-known definition is apparently more neutral: "Science fiction is that class of prose narrative treating of a situation that could not arise in the world we know, but which is hypothesised on the basis of some innovation in science or technology, or pseudo-science or pseudo-technology, whether human or extra-terrestrial in origin." The key to science fiction, Amis says, is that even when it deals with the implausible it attempts to conceal its implausibility. Thus differentiating science fiction from fantasy is easy, for it requires "little more than remarking that while science fiction, as I have been arguing, maintains a respect for fact or presumptive fact, fantasy makes a point of flouting these" (*New Maps of Hell: A Survey of Science Fiction*, New York: Harcourt, Brace, 1960, pp. 18-22). Do we not hear even in Amis' urbane voice an echo of Heinlein's combative note? The reasons for writers' uneasiness about science fiction, or at any rate about their audience's attitude toward science fiction, are interesting. Not only is science fiction generally regarded as a popular form and therefore in some sense as "escapist fantasy," but also, unlike detective or western fiction, it genuinely partakes of the fantastic. Science fiction suffers from a double opprobrium: it is doubly "not true." The strategy of most definitions is to assimilate science fiction to the dominant and culturally ap-

proved literary form, the realistic novel, and thus to rescue the genre from at least part of this opprobrium.

2. "On the Uses of Literary Genre," *Literature as System: Essays Toward the Theory of Literary History* (Princeton: Princeton University Press, 1971), p. 109.

3. Brian Aldiss makes the case for *Frankenstein* in *Billion Year Spree: The True History of Science Fiction* (Garden City: Doubleday, 1973). For recent historical surveys, see also James Gunn, *Alternate Worlds: The Illustrated History of Science Fiction* (Englewood Cliffs: Prentice-Hall, 1975), and Robert Scholes and Eric S. Rabkin, *Science Fiction: History, Science, Vision* (New York: Oxford University Press, 1977).

4. Unsigned review, *Critic*, April 1898, rpt. in Patrick Parrinder, ed., *H. G. Wells: The Critical Heritage* (London: Routledge and Kegan Paul, 1972), pp. 68–69. I. F. Clarke's valuable annotated bibliography, *The Tale of the Future from the Beginning to the Present Day*, 2nd ed. (London: Library Association, 1972), documents the marked rise in science-fiction activity in the last third of the nineteenth century. Particularly useful studies of this period include Thomas D. Clareson, "The Other Side of Realism," in his *SF: The Other Side of Realism* (Bowling Green: Bowling Green University Popular Press, 1971), pp. 1–28; the same author's "The Emergence of the Scientific Romance, 1870–1926," in Neil Baron, ed., *Anatomy of Wonder: Science Fiction* (New York: R. R. Bowker, 1976), pp. 33–78; and Mark R. Hillegas, "Victorian 'Extraterrestrials,'" in Jerome Buckley, ed., *The Worlds of Victorian Fiction* (Cambridge: Harvard University Press, 1975), pp. 391–414. On Chesney and the future-war theme, see I. F. Clarke, *Voices Prophesying War, 1763–1984* (London: Oxford University Press, 1966).

5. See Tzvetan Todorov, "The Origin of Genres," *New Literary History*, 8 (1976), 159–170: "From where do genres come? Why, quite simply, from other genres. A new genre is always the transformation of one or several old genres: by

inversion, by displacement, by combination" (p. 161).

6. For relevant discussions of romance, see Richard Chase, *The American Novel and Its Tradition* (Garden City: Anchor Press, 1957); Northrop Frye, "The Mythos of Summer: Romance," in *Anatomy of Criticism* (Princeton: Princeton University Press, 1957), pp. 186-206; Frye's development of his idea of romance in *The Secular Scripture: A Study of the Structure of Romance* (Cambridge: Harvard University Press, 1976); and Fredric Jameson, "Magical Narratives: Romance as Genre," *New Literary History*, 7 (1975), 135-163. Jameson's essay is important both as a discussion of romance and as a theoretical statement about the nature of genre.

7. *Seven Science Fiction Novels of H. G. Wells* (New York: Dover, n.d.), p. 34.

8. On the phases of generic development, see Alastair Fowler's "The Life and Death of Literary Forms," *New Literary History*, 2 (1971), 199-216.

9. *Out of the Silent Planet* (New York: Macmillan, 1978), pp. 29, 33.

10. *The Foundation Trilogy* (Garden City: Doubleday, n.d.), p. 45. Joseph F. Patrouch, Jr., notes this moment of self-consciousness; see *The Science Fiction of Isaac Asimov* (Garden City: Doubleday, 1974), pp. 70-71.

11. "Introduction," *The Left Hand of Darkness* (New York: Ace, 1976), n. pag.

12. See "Magical Narratives," esp. pp. 152-153.

13. The view of genre systems that I am suggesting depends on Saussure's fundamental distinction between *langue* and *parole*. For the application of Saussure's ideas to the concept of genre, see Claudio Guillén's "Literature as System," in *Literature as System*, pp. 375-419. Though Robert Scholes does not make an explicit distinction between generic ideas and texts, his discussion of science fiction in *Structural Fabulation: An Essay on the Fiction of the Future* (Notre Dame: University of Notre Dame Press, 1975) is in-

fluenced by the systematic concept of literature.

14. *The Castle of Otranto,* ed. W. S. Lewis (London: Oxford University Press, 1964), p. 7.

15. Cf. Robert M. Philmus' approach to science fiction as a rhetorical strategy of narrative presentation in *Into the Unknown: The Evolution of Science Fiction from Francis Godwin to H. G. Wells* (Berkeley and Los Angeles: University of California Press, 1970), esp. ch. 1. Clareson discusses the ideological relationship between the naturalistic movement and science fiction in "The Other Side of Realism." He sees science fiction as the optimistic contrary to the deterministic pessimism of naturalism. Both forms, he argues, are responses to the new age of science. On fantasy see C. N. Manlove, *Modern Fantasy* (Cambridge: Cambridge University Press, 1975); W. R. Irwin, *The Game of the Impossible: A Rhetoric of Fantasy* (Urbana: University of Illinois Press, 1976); and, particularly, Eric S. Rabkin, *The Fantastic in Literature* (Princeton: Princeton University Press, 1976), which deals with both science fiction and fantasy from a theoretical point of view. My conception of genre, but not my conception of fantasy or of the fantastic, has been greatly influenced by Tzvetan Todorov, *The Fantastic: A Structural Approach to a Literary Genre,* tr. Richard Howard (Cleveland: Case Western Reserve University Press, 1970).

16. See esp. "Aphasia as a Linguistic Topic," *Selected Writings* (The Hague: Mouton, 1971), II, 229–238; and "Two Aspects of Language and Two Types of Aphasic Disturbances," ibid., pp. 239–259.

17. See Darko Suvin's discussion of extrapolation and analogy in science fiction in his important theoretical essay "On the Poetics of the Science Fiction Genre," *College English,* 34 (1972), 372–383, and also his *Metamorphoses of Science Fiction: On the Poetics and History of a Literary Genre* (New Haven: Yale University Press, 1979), esp. pp. 27–30.

18. Scholes and Rabkin, *Science Fiction,* pp. 98-99: "Brian

Aldiss began his compendious history of science fiction with the assertion that 'science fiction doesn't exist.' The point may be debatable now, but if we put it in the proper tense — the future — it seems much less debatable. Science fiction will not exist. But the whole shape of literature will have changed." On the relationship between genre and mode, see Fowler, "Life and Death of Literary Forms," who argues that "genre tends to mode."

2 PARADIGM

1. *The Complete Short Stories of H. G. Wells* (London: Ernest Benn, 1948), pp. 644–655.

2. First developed by the Russian Formalists, the concept of *ostranenie,* estrangement, has been fruitfully applied to science fiction by Darko Suvin, who speaks of science fiction as "the literature of cognitive estrangement." See *Metamorphoses of Science Fiction: On the Poetics and History of a Literary Genre* (New Haven: Yale University Press, 1979), esp. pp. 3–15.

3. *The Science Fiction Hall Fame,* vol. 2–A, ed. Ben Bova (Garden City: Doubleday, 1973), p. 159.

4. *Nightwings* (London: Sphere Books, 1974), p. 7.

5. My formulation of the paradigm in terms of human and nonhuman merely makes explicit an understanding of science fiction that many, I expect, have shared. Edmund Crispin, for example, speaks of science fiction as characteristically showing man "in the presence of some *other* thing over which his control is partial or uncertain or in extreme cases nonexistent." This "Other Thing," Crispin continues, "is in some sense the definition of science fiction" (*Best SF Three;* London: Faber and Faber, 1958, pp. 10–11). In his excellent *The Known and the Unknown: The Iconography of Science Fiction* (Kent: Kent State University Press, 1979), Gary K. Wolfe deals with the issue in terms of the known and the unknown.

6. David Ketterer also excludes utopias from the genre, but on grounds somewhat different from my own. See his *New Worlds for Old: The Apocalyptic Imagination, Science Fiction, and American Literature* (Bloomington: Indiana University Press, 1974), esp. pp. 96–122. Ketterer is concerned with the internal structure of the genre. He proposes an archetypal plot that progresses through four phases: dystopian fictions, fictions of catastrophe, postcatastrophe stories, and fictions of other worlds. The pattern that informs science fiction is, in his view, that of the Book of Revelations: the destruction of one world and the revelation of another. Thus Ketterer gives priority to narrative pattern where I give priority to the playing field of a particular "semantic space." Naturally our results are different though not, I think, contradictory.

7. *Seven Science Fiction Novels of H. G. Wells,* p. 361.

8. *Science Fiction Hall Fame,* vol, 1, ed. Robert Silverberg (New York: Doubleday, 1970), p. 430.

9. John Huntington, "Science Fiction and the Future," *College English,* 37 (1975) 345–352, proposes that science fiction "answers a craving, not for a new and plausible technology, but for a science which will mediate between a conviction of the necessity of events – that is, a strict determinism – and a belief in a creative freedom." For a text analysis that nicely illustrates my argument, see Eric S. Rabkin, "Determinism, Free Will, and Point of View in Le Guin's *The Left Hand of Darkness,*" *Extrapolation,* 20 (1979), 5–19.

10. *Science and the Modern World* (New York: Free Press, 1967), esp. p. 76.

11. *Last and First Men and Star Maker* (New York: Dover, 1968), p. 183.

3 SPACE

1. See, for example, Georges Poulet, *Studies in Human Time,* tr. Elliott Coleman (Baltimore: Johns Hopkins University

Press, 1956), p. 13, whom I am paraphrasing here. Among the classic studies dealing with the disintegration of the Elizabethan World Picture are A. O. Lovejoy, *The Great Chain of Being* (Cambridge: Harvard University Press, 1936); Marjorie Hope Nicolson, *The Breaking of the Circle* (New York: Columbia University Press, rev. ed., 1960); and Alexandre Koyré, *From the Closed World to the Infinite Universe* (Baltimore: Johns Hopkins University Press, 1957).

2. Quoted by Charles Coulston Gillispie, *The Edge of Objectivity: An Essay in the History of Scientific Ideas* (Princeton: Princeton University Press, 1960), p. 26.

3. Quoted by Koyré, *From the Closed World to the Infinite Universe*, pp. 208–209. Koyré's study emphasizes Newton's religious belief and his indebtedness to Henry More.

4. Tennyson, "Vastness." On the Victorian crisis of faith and sense of loneliness and alienation, see Walter Houghton, *The Victorian Frame of Mind* (New Haven: Yale University Press, 1957), esp. pp. 27–180, and J. Hillis Miller, *The Disappearance of God* (Cambridge: Harvard University Press, 1963). Miller's opening chapter evokes the whole situation and also comments in passing on the inapplicability of the model of physical change to cultural history.

5. "The *Nautilus* and the Drunken Boat," *Mythologies,* tr. Annette Lavers (New York: Hill and Wang, 1972), pp. 65–67. Verne tends to be dismissed as a writer of adventure stories for boys. In France, however, he has lately been the subject of considerable critical attention and is becoming recognized as a major nineteenth-century writer. For an excellent general essay on Verne, see Michel Butor, "Le Point suprême et l'age d'or: A travers quelques oeuvres de Jules Verne," *Répertoire I* (Paris: Minuit, 1960), pp. 130–162. Marc Angenot surveys recent French studies in two articles both titled "Jules Verne and French Literary Criticism," *Science-Fiction Studies,* 1 (1973), 33–37, and 3 (1976), 46–49.

6. *Journey to the Centre of the Earth,* tr. Robert Baldick (Harmondsworth: Penguin Books, 1965), p. 47. Further citations are given in parentheses in the text. English translations of Verne being notoriously unreliable, I have checked the relevant passages in Baldick against the original in *Le Grand Jules Verne* published by Librairie Hachette.

7. In supposing the pole to be marked by a volcano opening into the earth's interior, Verne was employing the notions of the early nineteenth-century American proponent of the hollow-earth theory, John Cleves Symmes. Poe's *Narrative of Arthur Gordon Pym,* in which the seas become warm as the explorers approach the south pole, was probably also influenced by Symmes and was of course a major influence on Verne; see *The Narrative of Arthur Gordon Pym,* ed. Sidney Kaplan (New York: Hill and Wang, 1960), pp. xii–xiv.

8. Kenneth Allott calls Axel's dream "Verne's one poem: the complete marriage of romantic poetry and nineteenth century science"; see *Jules Verne* (Port Washington: Kennikat Press, 1970; reissue of 1954 ed.), p. 103. Allott's biography is an excellent study of Verne's relationship to the nineteenth-century context.

9. *Seven Science Fiction Novels of H. G. Wells* (New York: Dover, n.d.), p. 312. Further citations are given in parentheses in the text.

10. Samuel L. Hynes and Frank D. McConnell make a similar point about the bacteria in "*The Time Machine* and *The War of the Worlds:* Parable and Possibility in H. G. Wells," in *The Time Machine and The War of the Worlds: A Critical Edition,* ed. Frank D. McConnell (New York: Oxford University Press, 1977), pp. 345–366. McConnell's edition also reprints a number of standard discussions of Wells, including a selection from Bernard Bergonzi's important *The Early H. G. Wells* (Manchester: Manchester University Press,

1961), the study that remains the point of departure for criticism of Wells's science fiction. Valuable discussions of Wells's science fiction can also be found in *H. G. Wells: A Collection of Critical Essays,* ed. Bernard Bergonzi (Englewood Cliffs: Prentice-Hall, 1976), and in *H. G. Wells and Modern Science Fiction,* ed. Darko Suvin and Robert Philmus (Lewisburg: Bucknell University Press, 1977).

11. See John Huntington's excellent "The Science Fiction of H. G. Wells," in *Science Fiction: A Critical Guide,* ed. Patrick Parrinder (London: Longman, 1979), pp. 34–50.

12. See "The Alien Encounter: Or, Ms Brown and Mrs Le Guin," *Science-Fiction Studies,* 6 (1979), 46–58.

13. *The Mirror of Infinity,* ed. Robert Silverberg (New York: Harper and Row, 1973), p. 142.

14. *Solaris,* tr. Joanna Kilmartin and Steve Cox (New York: Berkley, 1971), p. 81. Further citations are given in parentheses in the text. The Kilmartin and Cox translation from the French, at two removes from the original Polish, may be untrustworthy on details, and I have tried to avoid arguments that depend upon a particular verbal formulation. In the Polish original, the character "Rheya" is evidently named "Harey," and "Snow" is "Snaut." See Edward Balcerzan's "Language and Ethics in *Solaris,*" *Science-Fiction Studies,* 2 (1975), 152–156. Among the other useful critical discussions of Lem are Darko Suvin's "The Open-Ended Parables of Stanislaw Lem and *Solaris,*" printed as an afterword to the text in the Berkley edition; David Ketterer's "*Solaris* and the Illegitimate Suns of Science Fiction," in his *New Worlds for Old: The Apocalyptic Imagination, Science Fiction, and American Literature* (Bloomington: Indiana University Press, 1974), pp. 182–202; and Jerzy Jarzebski, "Stanislaw Lem, Rationalist and Visionary," *Science-Fiction Studies,* 4 (1977), 110–126.

4 TIME

1. See Stephen Toulmin and June Goodfield, *The Discovery of Time* (New York: Harper and Row, 1965), pp. 84–86. On the Renaissance sense of time, see Ricardo J. Quinones, *The Renaissance Discovery of Time* (Cambridge: Harvard University Press, 1972), esp. ch. 1. Georges Poulet's classic *Studies in Human Time,* tr. Elliott Coleman (Baltimore: Johns Hopkins University Press, 1956), contains a brilliant introductory discussion of the perception of time from the Middle Ages to the present.

2. Quoted by Charles Coulston Gillispie, *The Edge of Objectivity: An Essay in the History of Scientific Ideas* (Princeton: Princeton University Press, 1960), p. 300.

3. See Toulmin and Goodfield, *The Discovery of Time,* pp. 169–170.

4. Quoted by Jerome Hamilton Buckley, *The Triumph of Time: A Study of the Victorian Concepts of Time, History, Progress, and Decadence* (Cambridge: Harvard University Press, 1966), p. 28.

5. On the pervasive historicism of the nineteenth century, see Walter Houghton, *The Victorian Frame of Mind* (New Haven: Yale University Press, 1957), *passim,* and Buckley, *The Triumph of Time.* Gerald L. Bruns, in "The Formal Nature of Victorian Thinking," *PMLA,* 90 (1975), 904–918, suggests how historical habits of mind shaped the form as well as the substance of nineteenth-century thought.

6. *The Sense of an Ending* (New York: Oxford University Press, 1967), esp. chs. 1–2.

7. Samuel L. Hynes and Frank D. McConnell contrast the spatiality of *The War of the Worlds* with the temporality of *The Time Machine.* See "*The Time Machine* and *The War of the Worlds:* Parable and Possibility in H. G. Wells," in *The Time Machine and The War of the Worlds: A Critical Edition,*

ed. Frank D. McConnell (New York: Oxford University Press, 1977), pp. 361–362.

8. *Seven Science Fiction Novels of H. G. Wells* (New York: Dover, n.d.), pp. 16, 67, 17–18. Further citations are given in parentheses in the text.

9. On the white sphinx and the color imagery, see David J. Lake, "The White Sphinx and the Whitened Lemur: Images of Death in *The Time Machine,*" *Science-Fiction Studies,* 6 (1979), 77–84.

10. On the creatures of the furthest future as human descendants, see Alex Eisenstein, "*The Time Machine* and the End of Man," *Science-Fiction Studies,* 3 (1976), 161–165.

11. *The Mirror of Infinity,* ed. Robert Silverberg (New York: Harper and Row, 1973), p. 219.

12. The best discussion of time travel is Stanislaw Lem's "The Time-Travel Story and Related Matters of SF Structuring," *Science-Fiction Studies,* 1 (1974), 143–154. Lem criticizes the tendency of science-fiction writers to remain at the level of pure intellectual play.

13. "The Past of Science Fiction," in *Bridges to Science Fiction,* ed. George E. Slusser, George R. Guffey, and Mark Rose (Carbondale: Southern Illinois University Press, 1980), pp. 131–146.

14. *A Canticle for Leibowitz* (New York: Lippincott, 1959), p. 245.

15. *Last and First Men and Star Maker* (New York: Dover, 1968), p. 15. Further citations are given in parentheses in the text.

16. *The Man in the High Castle* (New York: Berkley, 1974), pp. 43–44. Further citations are given in parentheses in the text. For good essays on Dick, see *Science-Fiction Studies,* 2 (1975), a special issue devoted to his work. Joseph Milicia's introduction to his reprint edition of *The Man in the High Castle* (Boston: Gress Press, 1979) is also useful.

17. *The Drowned World* (Harmondsworth: Penguin Books,

1965), p. 14. Further citations are given in parentheses in the text.

5 MACHINE

1. *Leviathan,* ed. A. R. Waller (Cambridge: Cambridge University Press, 1935), p. xviii. On the mechanistic world view and the romantic protest, see Alfred North Whitehead, *Science and the Modern World* (New York: Free Press, 1967), esp. chs. 4–5. Lewis Mumford's classic *Technics and Civilization* (New York: Harcourt, Brace, 1934) explores the relationship between the mechanistic world view and the industrial revolution.

2. "Signs of the Times," *Critical and Miscellaneous Essays* (New York: Scribners, 1904), II, 59. On early nineteenth-century pride in the power of machines, see Walter Houghton, *The Victorian Frame of Mind* (New Haven: Yale University Press, 1957), esp. pp. 198–201. Leo Marx's classic *The Machine in the Garden: Technology and the Pastoral Ideal in America* (New York: Oxford University Press, 1964) considers the response of American culture to the machine. Herbert L. Sussman's *Victorians and the Machine: The Literary Response to Technology* (Cambridge: Harvard University Press, 1968) is a useful study of the English response.

3. "The Nature of Gothic," *The Stones of Venice* (Boston and New York: Jefferson Press, n.d.) II, 162.

4. Marx, *Early Writings,* tr. and ed. T. B. Bottomore (New York: McGraw-Hill, 1964), pp. 122–123.

5. For a brilliant phenomenological discussion of *2001* in terms of bodies in movement, see Annette Michelson, "Bodies in Space: Film as 'Carnal Knowledge,'" *Artforum,* 7 (1969), 54–63. I am also indebted to Carolyn Geduld's *Filmguide to 2001: A Space Odyssey* (Bloomington: Indiana University Press, 1973). In passing let me note that Clarke's

novelization cannot be used to gloss the film. Repeatedly the novel provides explanations of elements that the film purposely leaves unexplained.

6. *The Invincible,* tr. Wendayne Ackerman (New York: Ace Books, n.d.), p. 218.

7. *The Best of Fredric Brown,* ed. Robert Bloch (Garden City: Nelson Doubleday, 1976), p. 112.

8. Among the more suggestive discussions of robots in the critical literature are Stanislaw Lem's "Robots in Science Fiction," in *SF: The Other Side of Realism,* ed. Thomas D. Clareson (Bowling Green: Bowling Green University Popular Press, 1971), pp. 307–325, and Gary K. Wolfe's "The Icon of the Robot" in his *The Known and the Unknown: The Iconography of Science Fiction* (Kent: Kent State University Press, 1979), pp. 151–183.

9. In Lem's collection *Mortal Engines,* tr. Michael Kandel (New York: Seabury Press, 1977), pp. 181–239.

10. *A Perfect Vacuum: Perfect Reviews of Nonexistent Books,* tr. Michael Kandel (New York: Harcourt Brace Jovanovich, 1979), p. 3. It should perhaps be noted that the context in which this statement appears is, to say the least, complex. By way of introduction to his collection of "reviews," Lem is reviewing his own book and he quotes this passage from the nonexistent "Introduction" to *A Perfect Vacuum* in order to criticize "Lem" for being long-winded and theoretical as well as for indulging in oversimplification. The self-reflexive irony is characteristic of Lem, but so is the statement.

11. *The Science Fiction Hall of Fame,* vol. 2–A, ed. Ben Bova (Garden City: Doubleday, 1973), p. 500.

12. As I mentioned in Chapter 2, utopian visions of the more fully human state are not generally perceived as science fiction. But one man's utopia is of course another's dystopia. Michael Holquist points out that society ceases to be a living organism in the utopia, becoming rather "a

machine for manufacturing that type of man which the author sees as the best man." See "How To Play Utopia: Some Brief Notes on the Distinctiveness of Utopian Fiction," *Yale French Studies,* 41 (1968), 106–123. The utopian writer naturally suppresses the mechanical nature of his state. The dystopian writer emphasizes it and thus produces a text in which society is projected as a nonhuman force. Containing within itself the potential for the dystopia, the utopian genre has been absorbed into science fiction through this process of inversion. In *Into the Unknown: The Evolution of Science Fiction from Francis Godwin to H. G. Wells* (Berkeley: University of California Press, 1970), Robert M. Philmus makes a point similar to my own about the place of the dystopian fable in the geography of science fiction. "What I am suggesting," Philmus writes, "is that the notion of the individual and the state as machines generates the myths of a number of twentieth-century science fantasies. By analyzing the cybernetic model and the dichotomies it entails, I have tried to supply the conceptual coordinates for mapping an important and extensive sector of modern science fiction" (p. 159).

13. *The Space Merchants* (New York: Ballantine Books, 1953), p. 75.

14. Written in Russian in 1920-21, *We* was first published in English in 1924. It has not to this day been published in the Soviet Union. Two English translations are in circulation, the original Gregory Zilboorg version of 1924 (New York: Dutton paperback) and a more recent version by Mirra Ginsburg (New York: Viking, 1972). My citations, which appear in parentheses in the text, refer to the Ginsburg version. The standard study of Zamiatin in English is Alex M. Shane, *The Life and Works of Evgenij Zamjatin* (Berkeley: University of California Press, 1968).

15. See Robert C. Elliott, "Literature and the Good Life: A Dilemma," *Yale Review,* 65 (1975), 24–37. Elliott's earlier *The*

Shape of Utopia: Studies in a Literary Genre (Chicago: University of Chicago Press, 1970) contains a good discussion of We.

16. Historically, the idea of utopia is associated with the idea of the city, and the city is the central image in most utopias and dystopias. See Lewis Mumford's "Utopia, The City and The Machine," in Utopias and Utopian Thought, ed. Frank E. Manuel (Boston: Houghton Mifflin, 1966), pp. 3–24. In "Myths of Origin and Destiny in Literature: Zamiatin's We," Extrapolation, 19 (1977), 68–75, Alexandra Aldridge develops the connection between Zamiatin's city and the New Jerusalem. On the city as an important science-fictional image, see Wolfe, The Known and the Unknown, pp. 86–124. Wolfe points out that the city is most often a negative image in science fiction, a barrier to human plenitude, as it is in We.

6 MONSTER

1. The literature concerned with self-alienation is vast. For an excellent general introduction to the idea, see "Alienation" in The Encyclopedia of Philosophy, ed. Paul Edwards (New York: Macmillan and Free Press, 1972), I, 76–81.

2. Hayden White's "The Forms of Wildness: Archaeology of an Idea," in The Wild Man Within: An Image in Western Thought from the Renaissance to Romanticism, ed. Edward Dudley and Maximillian E. Novak (Pittsburgh: University of Pittsburgh Press, 1972), pp. 3–38, analyzes the process of interiorization through which the notion of the wild man was transformed from an external to a psychic figure.

3. John Huntington makes this point in "The Science Fiction of H. G. Wells," in Science Fiction: A Critical Guide, ed. Patrick Parrinder (London: Longman, 1979), pp. 42–43.

4. On the figure of Proteus, see A. B. Giamatti, "Proteus Unbound: Some Versions of the Sea God in the Renaissance,"

in *The Disciplines of Criticism: Essays in Literary Theory, Interpretation, and History,* ed. Peter Demetz, Thomas Greene, and Lowry Nelson, Jr. (New Haven: Yale University Press, 1968), pp. 437–475.

5. *The Grotesque in Art and Literature,* tr. Ulrich Weisstein (Bloomington: Indiana University Press, 1963), p. 188.

6. On the daemonic see Angus Fletcher, *Allegory: The Theory of a Symbolic Mode* (Ithaca: Cornell University Press, 1964), pp. 25–69. Thomas H. Keeling discusses the daemonic in science fiction in "Science Fiction and the Gothic," in *Bridges to Science Fiction,* ed. George E. Slusser, George R. Guffey, and Mark Rose (Carbondale: Southern Illinois University Press, 1980), pp. 107–119. Keeling wants to distinguish between science fiction and the gothic, and thus his argument is somewhat different from my own.

7. See Edward Balcerzan, "Language and Ethics in *Solaris,*" *Science-Fiction Studies,* 2 (1975), 152–156.

8. See Gary K. Wolfe, *The Known and the Unknown: The Iconography of Science Fiction* (Kent: Kent State University Press, 1979). Wolfe's thesis is that science fiction continuously transforms the unknown into the known in an endless attempt to appropriate the infinite.

9. *The Mirror of Infinity,* ed. Robert Silverberg (New York: Harper and Row, 1973), p. 133.

10. See Thomas A. Hanzo's elegant discussion of these themes in "The Past of Science Fiction," in *Bridges to Science Fiction,* pp. 131–146.

INDEX

213

INDEX

INDEX

INDEX